PERSONAL BRANDING EXPERT   LINKEDIN BRANDING EXPERT
JANE ANDERSON & KYLIE CHOWN

CONNECT

LEVERAGE *your* LINKEDIN PROFILE *for* BUSINESS GROWTH *and* LEAD GENERATION

... IN LESS THAN

7 MINUTES PER DAY

Copyright © Jane Anderson and Kylie Chown 2015

ISBN 978-0-9942678-1-8

All rights reserved. No part of this book may be reproduced or transmitted in any form or by any means, electronic or mechanical, including photocopying (except under the statutory exceptions provisions of the Australian Copyright Act 1968), recording, scanning or by any information storage and retrieval system without the prior permission of the publisher.

Cover design, internal design and copy editing by Lauren Shay – Full Stop Design, Editing, Publishing.

"Over the past 100 years, we have moved from the Industrial Age, through the Information Age to the Digital Age. To thrive today, you need to be online and your expertise needs to be on show. Jane Anderson and Kylie Chown have shone a light on the path to having a digital presence on LinkedIn that really connects with your target audience and makes your expertise stand out. Clear, practical and simple, *CONNECT* is a must-read for anyone using LinkedIn to do business."
— *Dermot Crowley, Productivity Expert and author of "Smart Work", Wiley, 2015*

"The rules of connection have changed. We can connect and influence at the touch of a button and, as a result, our ability to manage our personal brand across multiple channels is critical. In this book, Jane and Kylie share how LinkedIn can build and leverage your brand to drive commercial and personal success. A must read packed with learnings, tools and tips for anyone wanting to take leadership of self."
— *Janine Garner, Collaboration Expert and author of "From Me to We", Wiley, 2015*

"*CONNECT* offers insights and practical tips on how to use LinkedIn to leverage your profile and business. Helping the reader work through at a strategic level what they want to be known for and then providing valuable guidance to achieve this. Put simply, if you have a LinkedIn profile and you are serious about your professional brand, then you must read this book."
— *Gabrielle Dolan, author of "Ignite: Real Leadership, Real Talk, Real Results", Wiley, 2015*

Acknowledgements

Thank you first and foremost to my parents, who are tireless supporters of me and my sisters. I am eternally grateful.

To Matt Church, Gabrielle Dolan, Janine Garner, Dermot Crowley, Patrick Hollingworth, Simon Waller, Rachel Bourke, Tracey Ezard, Dan Gregory and the rest of the Thought Leaders Global Community: thank you for your guidance, support and inspiration.

A special thank you to Keith Abraham. I am so grateful for your insights, care and interest. I feel very lucky to have you as a mentor.

Thank you to Lauren Shay, our editor. Your patience and guidance has made this work happen.

— *Jane Anderson*

Thank you to my parents and family. Your support and encouragement allow me to do what I do.

Thank you to the clients I work with. I appreciate that you are so open to sharing, and allow me to be part of your journey.

Thank you to Lauren Shay, our editor. Your work is amazing and we couldn't have done this without you.

— *Kylie Chown*

About the Authors

Jane Anderson

Jane Anderson is a LinkedIn and Personal Branding Expert. She has worked with more than 13,000 clients on marketing and to position them in their industries. Her clients include Rio Tinto, Virgin Australia, the Australian Medical Association, Origin Energy and various Thought Leaders, speakers and authors.

She has been featured in *Business Insider*, *The Age*, *Sydney Morning Herald*, *Marie Claire* and *Today Tonight*. She is also the author of *IMPACT: How to Build Your Personal Brand for the Connection Economy*.

When Jane's not travelling, speaking and running workshops, she lives in Brisbane, Queensland. She enjoys running, the beach and playing with her nieces and nephew.

- https://au.linkedin.com/in/janeandersonpersonalimpact
- www.jane-anderson.com

Kylie Chown

Kylie Chown is a LinkedIn and Digital Branding Expert. For more than 10 years, she has worked with start-ups, consultants and businesses to successfully leverage their LinkedIn profiles to their full capabilities.

Kylie has been featured as an expert in the *Australian Institute of Management (AIM)*, *Franchise Business*, *HRM America* and *Leaders in Heels*. She is also a regular guest on the *Reach Personal Branding* blog.

She is currently one of eight Certified Master Writers in Australia, and one of three Reach Certified Branding Analysts.

Kylie lives in Brisbane, Queensland, and when she's not working, she enjoys all that the Queensland lifestyle has to offer with her family and friends.

- https://au.linkedin.com/in/kyliechown
- www.kyliechown.com

Contents

Chapter 1: Why is LinkedIn So Important For You? — 1

Chapter 2: Where Are You Now? — 11

Chapter 3: How to Leverage Your Profile — 19

Chapter 4: Search Engine Optimisation (SEO) — 29

Chapter 5: Personal Branding — 77

Chapter 6: Connection — 111

Chapter 7: Organisational LinkedIn Strategy — 131

Chapter 8: Metrics vs Results — 147

Chapter 9: LinkedIn Groups — 153

Chapter 10: Company Pages — 157

Chapter 11: FAQs and Resources — 161

Chapter 1

Why is LinkedIn So Important For You?

Reid Hoffman, the co-founder of LinkedIn, recently said: "If you can get better at your job, you should be an active member of LinkedIn, because LinkedIn should be connecting you to the information, insights and people to be more effective."

In 2009, Jane began working with people on LinkedIn. It wasn't that LinkedIn was new; it was that it had been reserved for executives. She was helping people get jobs after the global financial crisis, and every so often she would meet someone who needed to be on LinkedIn. They were so reluctant to get online. She tried to find someone who could write their profiles. There wasn't anyone, so she began to write them herself.

Fast forward to 2011. Jane was on a plane next to a gentleman. She was flying between Brisbane and Canberra. She talked to the gentleman, and discovered he owned a technology company specialising in network security. He was also a professor of IT security at a university. He did a lot of consulting work in Canberra for the Australian Federal Government. Jane asked him: "Are all your team on LinkedIn? How do you use LinkedIn as part of your business?"

He said: "Actually, I've removed our sales team. I just have one sales manager now. I allow them to spend one day a week in forums on LinkedIn and other sites. Our technical experts answer questions and are connected to our customers. This is just how our customers want to communicate now, and our business has changed quite dramatically as a result."

Since then, we've noticed that traditional sales approaches and the new ways of selling and creating leads are quite different.

Most people will ask: "Isn't LinkedIn just like an online version of your resume?" Or: "Isn't it like Facebook, but for business?"

A LinkedIn profile is like your own personal website for your business and for you as someone in charge of sales or business growth. We're in the connection economy. When we're online, we want to be able to connect.

People do their research long before they get in touch with you. A CEB study found that about 60% of a buying decision is made before the person buys from you. It's a bit like TripAdvisor, where people do their research online before they decide to connect.

You can access people, information and misinformation more readily. If you need a financial planner and you're in Sydney, Australia, and you want to talk to someone in New York because you have been told they're the best, then that's what you can do. You're no longer restricted by location.

You can also access experts. Nowadays, if there is an expert in flamenco dancing and they are in Spain, you can go online and learn from a flamenco dancing teacher in Spain.

This is because of sites such as Elance, oDesk and Popexpert.

You might be thinking, "What does that have to do with LinkedIn?" What it means is that if you focus locally, you must have a strong presence, and LinkedIn is an effective way of achieving that.

It's getting more difficult to access decision makers because they're so busy. According to a study by the Radicati Group, business users sent and received on average 121 emails a day in 2014, and this is expected to grow to 140 emails a day by 2018. The amount of information landing in inboxes is extraordinary.

To cut through this noise is quite difficult, so we have to go to spaces where people hang out. Considering the average person spends two hours per day using social media, this is where we need to go to connect with them. We are in the connection economy.

The truth is we don't even know about missed opportunities because we don't get feedback.

Challenges with the Current Sales Process

Pigeonholing, Stereotypes and Unconscious Bias

You would have heard the saying: "first impressions last". In fact, Margaret Thatcher once said: "I usually make a decision about a person in the first 10 seconds and I usually find that I'm right."

There is a lot of information and misinformation out there. People want to understand who you are and where you're coming from. Otherwise, they will stereotype you very quickly. Their perception could be based on what you have done in the past, rather than what you can offer for the future.

You need to determine what you want their interpretation of you to be, and convey yourself in that light when you connect. They may not need your help right now, but they may know someone who does.

Something to remember is that your mistakes are not as obvious online as they are in the real world and you don't know the opportunities you're missing. People can look at your profile and move on, and you don't even know. There is a world of opportunity sitting at your fingertips. It's now time to take the opportunity to help those clients who are looking for you and need your help!

Some other challenges in the current selling climate include:

- **Access to decision makers:** This is more difficult as gatekeepers are becoming more challenging to manage.
- **"Digital First":** Increasingly customers are undertaking research online before making buying decisions. As mentioned, 60% of a buying decision is made before a customer makes contact. This means the use of Google searches are increasing. Sites such as Trip Advisor to choose hotels and Urban Spoon to choose a restaurant are examples of that.
- **The high cost of doing business:** Organisations are finding it increasingly challenging to meet skyrocketing overheads and wages. Businesses don't have money to waste any more.
- **Flexibility:** Businesses need to be able to move fast. Customers' needs change quickly and businesses need to be agile, yet stay on track.
- **The struggle to find more ideal customers:** It's difficult for businesses to position themselves for new clients and markets.
- **Time and money:** A business's growth isn't restricted to a local area anymore. We have access to markets nationally an internationally, but it takes time and money to build those markets and have a presence in those locations.
- **Unqualified leads:** We don't have time to waste on people who don't meet your sales criteria.
- **People do their research:** Customers research online to find the cheapest option.
- **The increasing cost of search engine optimisation and Google AdWords:** It's becoming extraordinarily expensive to get results from online advertising.
- **A feeling of paralysis:** With the sea of information available, combined with a lack of time and money, many businesses choose to do nothing. It can all seem too hard.

The Connection Economy

The old ways of selling have changed. It used to be about calling. It used to be about samples and then trying to get meetings with people. Now it's quite different. Now it's about leveraging people's social networks. It's about engagement, which means connecting with people, and it's about education. We need to be able to educate people about how we can help them. This is, essentially, the social sales model.

Past	Present	Future
Employees	Role Models	Ambassadors
Cold Calls	Tribes	Engagement
Sales Demonstrations	Education	Thought Leadership
Salesperson	Trusted Adviser	Expert
Transaction	Solution Selling	Lifetime Partnership

According to Ipsos Open Thinking Exchange, the average person spends two hours a day on the internet. IBM's Global CEO Study found that CEOs believe social media utilisation for customer engagement will increase by 256% over five years to become the second-most popular way to engage customers after face-to-face communication.

How You're Found in the Marketplace

Customers find you via various means when they work with you. The following quadrants are the most common.

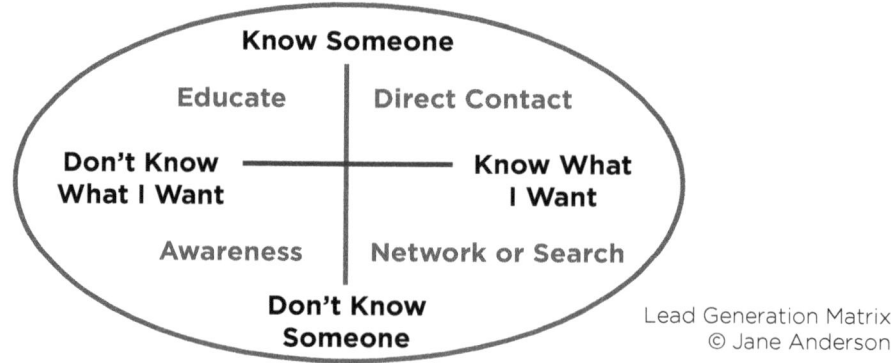

Lead Generation Matrix
© Jane Anderson

So, How Do People Find You?

"If I know someone and I don't know what I want."
If this is the case with a customer, they're going to ask the people they know. If they're more extroverted, they will probably go to their networks. If they're more introverted, then they will jump online and do a Google search.

The benefit of being referred in your networks means you have a good reputation. If you've got a good reputation, then you've got good positioning.

The problem with someone doing a Google search is that they don't know you, so you will be competing against others who have experience with search engine optimisation or Google AdWords. What it also means is that you will be like toothpaste on a supermarket shelf, looking the same as everybody else. You will compete on price, and that's a very difficult space in which to sell.

If you are well networked, then your referrals will come to the fore and that can be more effective.

"If I know someone and I know what I want, then what I'm going to do is direct contact."
If this is the case, the customer is going to pick up the phone and call you or email you because they already know who you are. The challenge for direct contact is that you have to be front of mind.

"For someone I don't know and I don't know what I want."
In that case, your job is to educate. You have to make sure you're putting content out there so people understand what you do and realise that they do have a particular problem. If someone has a problem, they're not going to know unless you keep educating them. You want them read your content and think, "There, that's exactly what I'm after."

"I don't know that I have a problem and I don't know someone."
In that case, your job is awareness. Your job is to make sure your profile is clear about how you help people, but you also must write blog posts and articles to help people become aware of the type of work you do. They might not need your help right now, but down the track they may realise there's a problem they need solving.

So the challenge is that we need to work on all quadrants of the Lead Generation Matrix. Yes, those who already know you make your job easy, but remember that someone out there is trying to find you, even if they don't know it yet.

What Type of LinkedIn Lead Generator Are You?

	BLACK-BELT LINKEDIN LEAD GENERATOR		
	TYPE	FOCUS	% LEAD GENERATION
ATTRACT	Ninja	Sales Maker	100
ATTRACT	Influencer	Thought Leader	85
ATTRACT	Active	Curator	70
ATTRACT	Positioned	Expert	50
REPEL	Resume	Commodity	10
REPEL	Account	Lost	5
REPEL	No Account	Judged	-10

© Jane Anderson 2015

Repel

Level 1 – No account. At this level, you'll be judged; judged that you're not up with the times or stereotyped in a way that may not be true. If you have no social media account, especially if you have no LinkedIn profile, you won't be seen as managing your presence. If you don't manage your brand, someone else will.

Level 2 – Account. This may be where a LinkedIn account came about unexpectedly for you. You didn't ask for an account but someone invited you, so you set one up. You haven't entered any information. It's an empty profile, with just your name and current position, and possibly a previous role. At least you're on LinkedIn, but it's not helping you or your organisation.

Level 3 – Resume. Your profile contains your career history and the tasks you did in your previous roles. Your summary is more about you and less about how you help your customer. With a profile that seems more like an obituary, you come across as a commodity in the market of talent instead of an expert in your field. You appear vanilla and boring, the same as everyone else, which is untrue.

Attract

Level 4 – Positioned. Your profile is written for your future and designed to attract the right people. When people land on your profile, it's clear who you help and you are positioned as an expert in your industry. There is nothing untrue in how your profile is written; it matches the human being and ensures the reader categorises you correctly without making assumptions.

Level 5 – Active. You're positioned and starting to become more active with your profile. You feel confident about liking, sharing and commenting on posts that are linked to what you're trying to achieve. You don't like or share anything that doesn't relate to your purpose.

Level 6 – Influencer. You are now creating original content and posts that link to your strategy. People are starting to follow you and like what you're saying. A tribe might even be forming and you're seeing the same people like and comment on your posts. Your profile may get 50-150 views per week. You're seeing more clients coming to you, wanting to do business.

Level 7 – Ninja. You're now leveraging your profile to create connections and open doors. You have specific scripts that you use to gain meetings with potential clients. You're starting to have more clout to ask for what you want as you've been contributing to your audience. You know how to move potential clients through your sales funnel.

Why LinkedIn?

With more than 365 million users, LinkedIn is a great opportunity to grow a business in front of a highly targeted audience. It was originally created for executives only, but it has grown to connect professionals at all levels – even graduates, who are the fastest-growing LinkedIn demographic. The most under-represented group is women, and this presents one of the greatest opportunities online.

LinkedIn was developed in 2003 by Reid Hoffman. He organised a team from PayPal and SocialNet to work on the idea. Growth was slow to begin with, some days only attracting 20 people at a time. Fast-forward to 2009 when Jeff Weiner, previously an executive at Yahoo!, took the reins as CEO while Hoffman managed product development. By the end of 2010, LinkedIn had 90 million members and 1000 employees around the world. By 2013, it had reached 225 million members, acquiring two members per second. Today, it has more than 7600 employees and is listed on the stock exchange. The site is available in 24 languages and has members listed in more than 200 countries. In 2015, LinkedIn acquired Lynda.com for $1.5 billion.

LinkedIn doesn't seem to be going anywhere any time soon. It has had a dramatic impact on the way business is done in the digital world and has been a game changer for professionals and businesses.

Fears of Using LinkedIn for Business Growth, Lead Generation and Networking

Time and Return on Investment

One fear people have about LinkedIn is how much time it will take out of their day. "Are you going to say that I have to sit on LinkedIn for half an hour a day or 20 minutes a day? I just don't have that kind of time." Definitely not. That's not a good use of time for a lot of. In some areas, such as business development and sales teams, it is a good use of time, but for most other roles it's about getting the profile written correctly and leveraging it to support other business activities.

Loss of Talent

One of the other fears leaders have about LinkedIn is that well-written profiles will lead to recruiters poaching their organisation's talent. If that happens, it means the profile has been written incorrectly. The LinkedIn profile-writing strategy for a team member versus a job seeker is very different. It is a different process, with a different result. If the profile is written based on what the organisation wants to achieve, then it won't appear in talent pools and it will be clear to a recruiter that the team member is not looking for a job.

Looking Stupid

Many clients we work with have a fear of looking stupid or failing to manage their profile successfully. They may also be concerned about not knowing how to handle the situation if they post something online that people disagree with.

Competitors

Some people are concerned that their competition will use LinkedIn to see what they're doing. "What if they try to steal my clients? How do I protect my connections, my clients and myself?"

So What's This Really About?

Connection

As humans, we have an innate need to belong. Our sense of community and tribe dictates our self-esteem. In today's digital world, it supports our need for connection through sites such as Facebook, Twitter, Instagram and LinkedIn.

People Buy From People

People buy from people, and they buy from people they know, like and trust. This marketing speak has been going around for years, but it is amplified in the connected and social-network economy.

Accessibility

If you have built a website, you may find it takes a few weeks to index correctly with Google. This has a high impact on your business if you're sitting and waiting for enquiries via your website. LinkedIn's indexing generally takes two days, so you can be found in a Google search much faster.

Experts

If you aren't positioning yourself effectively to your market, someone else is. Your expertise needs to be accessible to your market via blogs, videos, books and podcasts. LinkedIn is the perfect place to leverage your thought leadership.

24/7

Waiting to get in contact with people or doing your research by making phone calls doesn't work anymore. With websites, Facebook and LinkedIn, businesses are now open to the public 24/7 and marketing needs to be able to reach customers in the hours that suit them. Clients respond to emails at 2am and on Sundays. We no longer work 9-5 and no longer have a work-life balance. It's just life.

Low Cost

We live in a global – not just a local – marketplace. The internet has opened access to experts across the world on oDesk, Elance, Popexpert, Facebook and LinkedIn. Accessing experts in other countries used to be expensive, but we can now work with experts around the world at a competitive price.

Rely on Search

By purely relying on a Google search to get clients, you risk minimising your positioning. You become like toothpaste on the supermarket shelf, where people are trying to decide which one to buy but they're not sure, so they just buy the one on special. You need to stand out to maximise your positioning in the market and show what makes you different.

Connection

This is about being found for what you want to be found for, and creating networks and leads. It's about being positioned correctly in your client's mind so that leads convert to sales more easily. As Seth Godin in *Tribes* says, your network becomes your greatest asset for business growth.

Reflections and Actions

- How much does your marketing currently cost?
- How are you measuring the success of those activities?
- How do you manage your face-to-face relationships online?
- How do you educate your tribe?

Chapter 2

Where Are You Now?

Bill Owens, the 40th Governor of Colorado, once said: "We know that, when it comes to technology and the economy, if you're not constantly moving forward, then – without a doubt – you're moving backwards."

LinkedIn can seem like a huge beast and knowing where to start can be bewildering. This leads to procrastination and putting it into the too-hard basket. You may feel frustrated because you know there is an opportunity there, but you don't know how to make the most of it.

Furthermore, perhaps you don't want to use LinkedIn for selling but as a positioning tool when networking. People can view your profile for validation after face-to-face activity, such as attending events. You may also want to use your profile as a way of validating yourself as a leader if you're advertising a job for a new team member.

You

Is LinkedIn right for you?

Just having a profile for the sake of it is no reason to have one. At the moment, it might be a validator for you more than a business development tool.

Bridget Loudon, the CEO of Expert 360, an online brokerage site matching management consultants with clients across the world, tells a story about her parents, who live in South Africa, and her grandmother, who lives in Newcastle. Her parents were trying to find the right surgeon to help her grandmother who had a shoulder injury. They conducted their research for a surgeon in Newcastle from their home in South Africa.

In terms of your profile, you need to think outside your immediate surroundings and immediate location. Someone, somewhere in the world is trying to find you. We are not in a local marketplace any more. We're in a global marketplace and you need to be easily validated by people who can't physically see you or who aren't familiar with you.

LinkedIn is right for you if you:

- Have your own business
- Clients ask for you
- Are the leader of an organisation or school
- Are in business development or sales
- Are a consultant, trainer, coach, facilitator or an expert in your field
- Have the type of business that is reactive
- Rely on Google searches for clients

For example, if you have a pest control business, you could pay Google AdWords $10 – $10.50 for a click-through from a Google page. Your profile could still be well validated if you have a good relationship with real estate agents or property managers. It can still complement your business, even if you're not necessarily using it for aggressive business and sales growth. People buy from people and they buy from people they know, like and trust. In the LinkedIn field, this will mostly be business to business, but it can also be used for business to consumer, especially for referrals. For example, if I'm a personal trainer, my clients may be on LinkedIn, so it can be easier for them to refer me to their friends. They can get a feel for who I am far more quickly on LinkedIn than Facebook, especially if I'm not connected to my friends at work on Facebook.

When a potential client needs help, they will either ask their networks or undertake a search. You need to make sure your business turns up in both those cases easily. For example, if I hurt myself and I need to see a chiropractor, I will more than likely Google "Chiropractor Brisbane" and rely on the website that comes up. You can also use your LinkedIn profile to come up in the same search.

Metrics for Measuring Where You Are Now

All-Star Status

You may notice you have an area on your profile that shows if you have an "All-Star" status. This means that your profile has been fully completed. If it doesn't say "All-Star", then you need to fill your profile with more content. Bear in mind, though, that having an "All-Star" status doesn't mean you have an effective profile. It just means the fields have been completed.

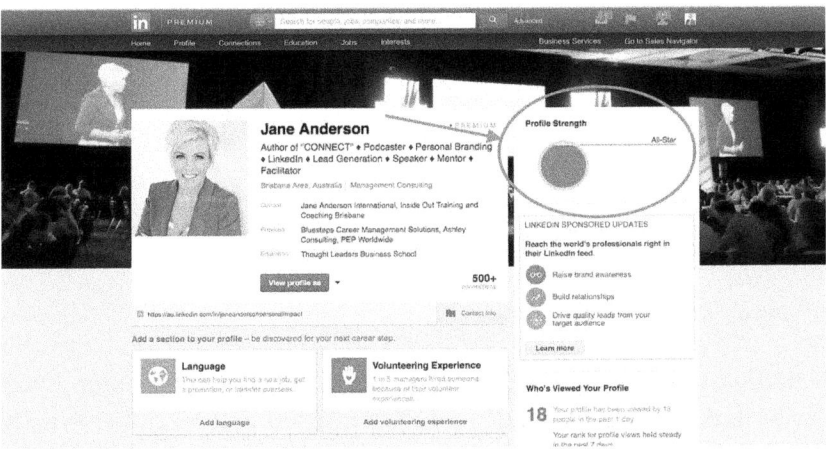

Visibility and Who Viewed Your Profile

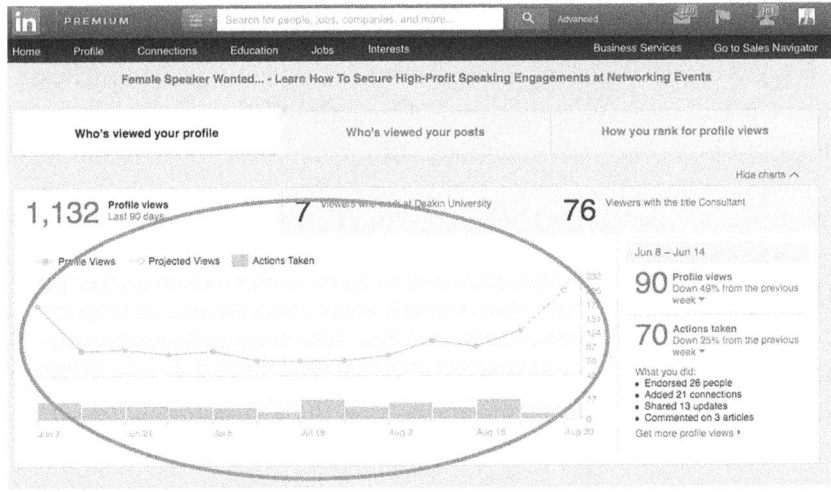

If you have a Premium Account, you may notice a graph in the "Who Viewed Your Profile" area that shows a line of how many people viewed your profile and, in the bar graph underneath, the action that was taken. If your line graph is going up but your bar graph is consistently going down, this may mean that your content is not relevant to your audience. If the line is going down but the bar graph is going up, this means the right person is looking at your profile. So a line going down isn't always a bad sign.

How You Rank for Profile Views

You'll also notice this option that shows you how you rank in your connections. Many people place a lot of importance on this. However, it depends on who you're connected to. If you're an IT salesperson and you're connected with lots of other IT sales people, you will rank low. If you're the only IT salesperson in your connections, you will rank highly. There are too many factors to take into consideration to lose a lot of time managing this metric.

How to Manage an Out-of-Control Account

"It is just bringing me more work, work I don't have time for."

We recently worked with a client who was a human resources manager. During the consultation, we talked about LinkedIn and he revealed that he didn't even log in to his LinkedIn account as "it is just bringing me more work, work I don't have time for."

He talked about how his inbox was being flooded with requests to connect and suppliers wanting his company's business. He saw LinkedIn as a medium that brought him more work and people wanting things from him. He didn't know how to control his account so he could use it to his benefit.

This client is not alone. A recent article on infoworld.com quoted professional developer Peter Wayner as saying this about LinkedIn: "It's sure cool and it's fun to look at hierarchies, but I've never had much luck with using it for more than idle curiosity."

David Linthicum, consultant and chief technology officer at Blue Mountain Labs, has a much more positive spin. He uses LinkedIn several times a day. He says: "I use LinkedIn to get the information on people I may want to work with, may want to hire, may want to network with. Most people in IT have LinkedIn profiles, and you can understand a lot about them from their profile." He has a problem with the site, though: "I get many people asking me to join their network who turn out to be spammers. You have to be careful who you accept."

Some ways to take control of your LinkedIn account and have it work for you include:

1. **Control your settings.** By controlling your settings, you can take control of incoming communication notifications and emails. To do this: Under the **Privacy and Settings** option, you will see you have five main areas you can manage. These include: Profile; Communications; Group, Companies and Applications; and Account.

2. **Manage your current connections.** You can keep your connections private. The default LinkedIn setting is that your first-degree connections can see who your other first-degree connections are. By making your connections private, you protect yourself and your connections. You can also block a connection's status updates if you still want to be connected, but don't want to see all their updates.

3. **Curb your connection requests.** Carefully review any requests to connect. Inadvertently connecting with a spammer can compromise your account. You can also control who can connect with you by stipulating that they need to have your email address to submit a connection request. When someone requests a connection, you will receive an email as well as a notification in your profile. If you click on the tick, the request will be accepted. If you would like to find out more about the person, click on their name.

Google Search

If you do a search for your profile in LinkedIn using keywords, you will turn up in the search result as the top-ranked profile, as LinkedIn search results are based on first, second and third-level connections. To get a real indication of where you're turning up in search results, you need to undertake a "clean search". You do need to be mindful of whether you're reviewing a public or individual profile.

LinkedIn public profiles come in two different formats: they start with www.linkedin.com/in/ or they start with www.linkedin.com/pub/

If there is an "in" in the URL this means the user has a premium subscription profile. "Pub" is for everyone else.

For example, if you were looking for a **LinkedIn Profile Writer** in Brisbane you would undertake the following search:

"site:linkedin.com/in | site:linkedin.com/pub -dir "LinkedIn Profile Writer" Brisbane"

By doing this search you get all profiles returned regardless of whether they have paid for a premium account or not.

How People Find You

When assessing how people find you, you need to consider the purpose and patterns that lead to how you're found. Some of the patterns come from your contacts and who you're connected to. You may notice certain people keep looking at your profile and coming back to you that way. They may have also found you more easily if you've been undertaking aggressive search engine optimisation with your profile.

The amount of content you post will also affect how you're found and will give evidence of your visibility. The best way to review this is by looking through your newsfeed.

So the overall message is that you don't need to place high in search results for everything. It depends on your purpose and who your connections are.

Self-Assessment

Here is a checklist with some questions to help you determine if your LinkedIn profile is working for you and where you need to focus your efforts.

	Current score /10	Final score /10
Establish Your Profile		
1. Does your profile address the problems and fears of your ideal client?		
2. Do you have a professional headshot?		
3. Do you control updates clogging your inbox?		
4. Is your profile fully search engine optimised in the title, summary, current role, skills and expertise, and does it include a vanity URL and contact details?		
5. Are you well validated with recommendations and endorsements?		
Total score /50		
Engage Your Audience		
6. Do you like and comment professionally?		
7. Do you create personalised scripts to connect professionally?		
8. Do you leverage LinkedIn to support your face-to-face networks?		
9. Do you curate content in a time-efficient and relevant manner?		
10. Do you contribute to groups professionally?		
Total score /50		
Elevate Your Positioning		
11. Do you undertake advanced searches to find ideal connections?		
12. Are you positioned effectively when being introduced to a potential client or contact?		
13. Can you write a thought-leading post with a call to action to attract ideal clients?		
14. Do you know how to write a compelling script to connect with ideal stakeholders via Connect or InMail, knowing the difference between the two?		
Total score /40		
Empower Your Team		
15. Can you maintain and troubleshoot your profile?		
16. Do you know how to run your business page?		
Total score /20		
TOTAL SCORE /160		

Reflections and Actions

- Your score from the above activity will determine the actions you need to take in this book. Focus your efforts on where you have gaps and go to the chapter that relates to that area, so you can find out what you need to do to get a score of 10.
- Consider your Google search. Google yourself and see where you turn up in that search. If a current or potential client found it, would it be a favourable result?
- How many views per week do you currently get on your LinkedIn profile? Take a screen grab and record it.
- Give yourself a pat on the back for those areas where you have already scored 10 out of 10!

Chapter 3

How to Leverage Your Profile

Hollywood actress Hilary Duff once said: "I'm pretty good at thinking about everything – all of my consequences – before I make a decision, and I think about everything that's going to happen because of that decision. I'm a Libra, and I'm very strategic."

We recently worked with a client, Peter, in financial services, who said he was spending a lot of time trying to grow his business through LinkedIn but found he was wasting so much time that he gave up and decided to just focus on his old sales methods. He couldn't understand what he was doing wrong on LinkedIn, so he dismissed it. Maybe you have been in the same boat, where you have tried to use LinkedIn but received minimal results. The goal of this book is to help you have greater impact in as short amount of time as possible. A good place to start is to think about the type of user you are before beginning.

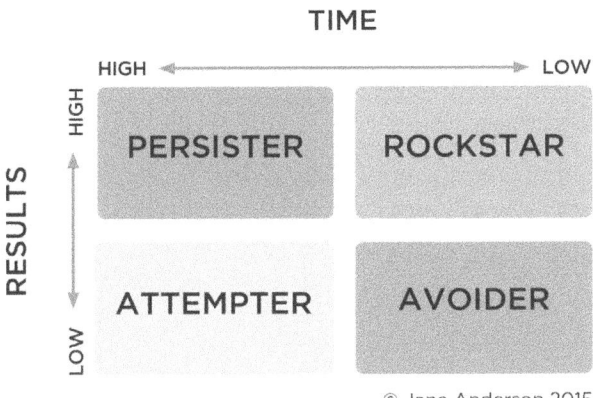

Q1: Persister. You're getting results but it's taking a lot of time. You're posting content but unsure if it's the right content. You feel as though there must be a better way but you're not sure what that is. You'd like to know some more efficient ways to make your profile work and be less time consuming. If you're at this level, you need to focus on efficiency, effectiveness and getting your profile to work for you a lot more. You may also need to look at the sequence of what you're doing with your profile. The order of your activity may also be out of sequence and need to be adjusted.

Q3: Attempter. You've tried putting some time into your LinkedIn profile but you're not getting any results. You're about to give up if something doesn't change. You feel overwhelmed and it all seems too hard. At this level, you need to focus on creating the strategy for your profile that will create the results you're looking for. You also need to shift from the mindset of taking from others to giving to generate leads.

Q4: Avoider. You think LinkedIn is more a recruitment tool. You may think that if profiles are created for your team, they will leave and not attract clients. You have a private profile because you don't want attention and you don't see yourself as an integral part of the sales funnel. Alternatively, you don't have time to spend on social media and don't even see the value of it. If you're at this level, you need to look at the purpose of your role in the organisation and where LinkedIn's purpose intersects. From here, your strategy can be designed to leverage the time you spend on it and keep you focused on business-critical activity.

Q2: Rockstar. You're confident and killing it. You know how to design your profile to attract your ideal client. You're leveraging your content, approaching your clients with ease and generating leads. You know the process, have the system in place and it's a strategic part of your sales process. You know there is no replacement for face-to-face communication, but you know how to leverage LinkedIn to support other lead-generating activities. At this level, you can focus on helping others in your business or elevating the business through your profile and other thought-leadership activities.

There are three elements to get help you move to Rockstar Status:

- Search Engine Optimisation
- Positioning
- Connection

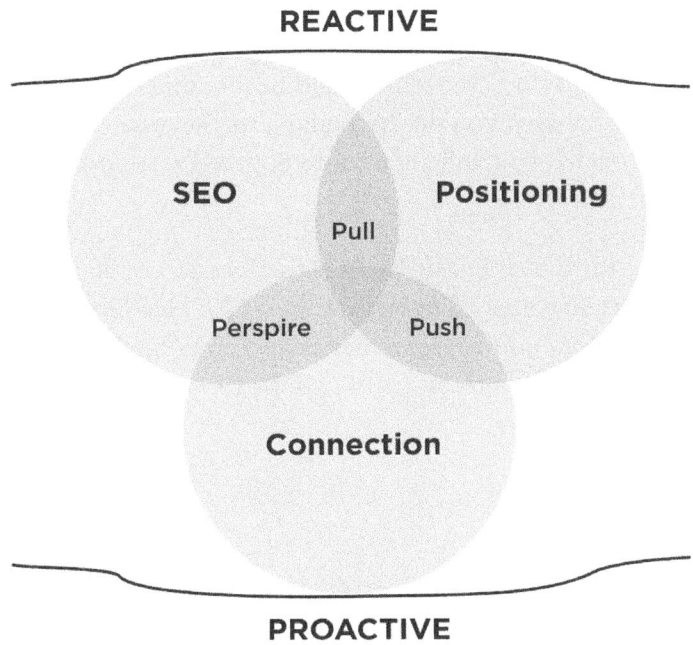

Search Engine Optimisation

LinkedIn, first and foremost, is a search engine. In other words, it's similar to Google in that it's designed for people to use to search for what they're looking for. Not only does this mean that you can turn up in a search result in LinkedIn; you can also turn up in a Google search if you have the right words in your profile. The advantage of this is that you can beat your competitors, even if they're large organisations, in a Google as well as a LinkedIn search.

So, one of the first things you need to have in your profile is search engine optimisation, or SEO. SEO is about having the correct words in your profile so that you turn up in search results and are found. There are three main elements to keep in mind when search engine optimising your profile:

1. **Relevance:** Ensure you use words that a customer uses when searching for you. For example, if you're a facilitator in leadership, a customer could type in "Leadership Facilitator Sydney", but there are also people who might type in "Leadership Trainer Sydney" or "Leadership Training Sydney". Ensuring you have enough of the words in your profile means that people can find you for what you want to be found for. By doing this, your profile will have a lot of pull. This means your profile will bring the right people to you like a magnet.

2. **Competitiveness:** Some keywords will be more competitive than others. This means that to get a strong, targeted result, you may need to be more specific. For example, the keyword "coach" would be a competitive keyword. It is also not very specific to what you do. By making the keyword "junior AFL coach" or "executive coach", you will get a more targeted response that aligns with your goals and ideal client.

3. **Location:** The third element of SEO is the location of keywords in your profile. There are five areas that impact the SEO: Headline, Summary, Employment History and Endorsements Recommendations. Ensure you include your keywords in all areas to maximise your SEO.

Positioning

When you have positioning, it means you stand out from your competition. You have differentiated yourself from others and you are perceived in the market for the work you want to be perceived as being able to do.

The main elements of positioning are:

1. **Content:** Your content relates to your expertise; it relates to those things that help your audience to understand what you do to help. It's about your profile photo, your content and your thought leadership. It's about your brand leverage and being the brand of the companies you have worked for.

2. **Social Proof:** What others say about you is more important than what you say about yourself. The importance of testimonials and case studies cannot be over emphasised. The evidence that you can do what you say you can do is invaluable and gives people hope as well as trust in you.

3. **First Four Seconds:** When a client lands on your profile, they don't make a cup of tea and read your profile, taking in every captivating word. You only have four seconds to grab their attention and help them make sense of what you do. Your profile needs to stand out immediately!

Connection

One of the things we often hear people say about LinkedIn is: "I've got a profile, but it doesn't do anything for me." It's actually a bit more of a team effort. People set up their profile thinking, "Oh, it's done now. I'll just sit back and wait." You need to be proactive with your profile, but there's no point being proactive unless you've got full SEO and it's fully branded. Only then can you go to market.

Just because you're online rather than engaging face-to-face doesn't mean you should treat people any differently. It can be easy to forget that the people behind the computer screen are human. The As a result of the sheer volume of people online, we try to speed everything up to attract the masses. The irony is that this slows the process down. The secret is less haste, more speed.

The three elements of connection are:

1. **Strategy (What):** What do you want to be doing with your clients? What do you help them with? What value do you bring? What problems do your customers have that you are trying to solve? For example, if you're a school principal, you're solving a parent's issue of deciding what school to enrol their child in. If you're an executive coach, you're helping people with their confidence or work-life balance. You're solving their problem of feeling burnt out and helping them regain their energy to re-connect to their work.

2. **Leads (Who):** The connection part is about knowing who you want to work with, so that your profile generates leads and puts you in front of the right people. If you're not able to move to a face-to-face or phone conversation, then you're not moving people to the next step. Clients don't magically appear from nowhere and buy from you. You need to make it easy for them to have a conversation with you.

3. **Responses (How):** What do you say when you want to connect with others or when they want to connect with you? Do you just use the default settings LinkedIn gives you? Do you know how to create a script that you use with potential clients? By personalising your interactions, you will move much more quickly than you will by just using what LinkedIn gives you. Default settings make people feel like a commodity; that you don't really care and you're just in it for you.

Push, Pull and Perspire

Our goal is to get both Push and Pull working in harmony with the least amount of Perspiration. If you have nothing in your profile, you will get nothing. If you have the right words and language in your profile, you're more likely to attract people who want those services.

Your push strategy is designed to complement that, so that when people land on your profile, they say: "Oh wow! I definitely want to talk to you."

Push comes from being able to put your content out there. Pushing content supports the pull strategy. A real direct push is about approaching people directly.

Take Control

Connecting with people on LinkedIn is a bit like dating. If you decide to lock yourself in your house and say, "Well, one day Prince Charming's going to turn up at my front door," then it's not going to happen.

You need to make some effort to reach out and connect with people. To do that, you need to:

- Know what you want and who you're going to connect with.
- Pre-write your scripts. Make sure you know what you're going to say when you go to connect with people.

Decide if you're going to connect by standard connection or InMail. This will be dependent on your budget, the amount of characters you're going to use and if you have a premium account.

People buy when they're ready. Your job is to ensure you're the person they contact when they need help. Overall, there are three things you need to be doing with your profile:

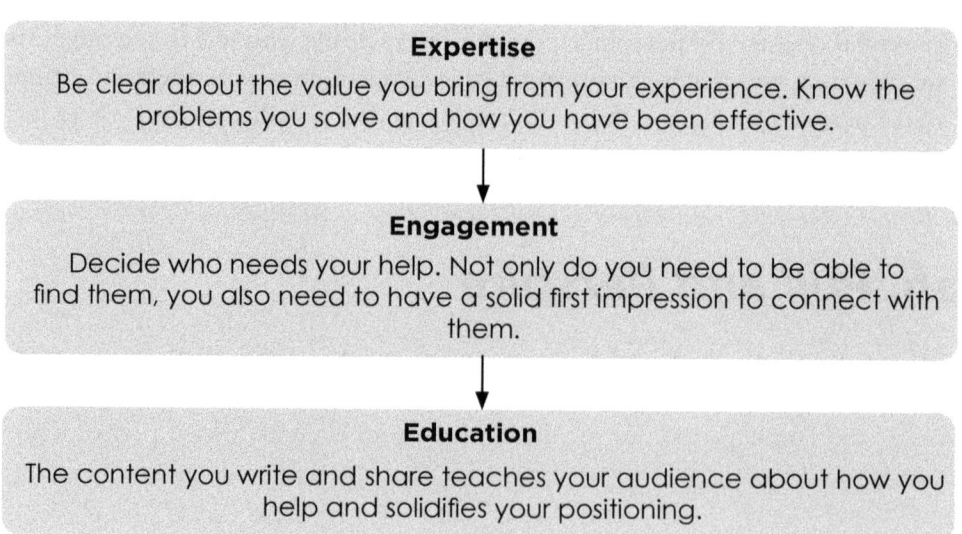

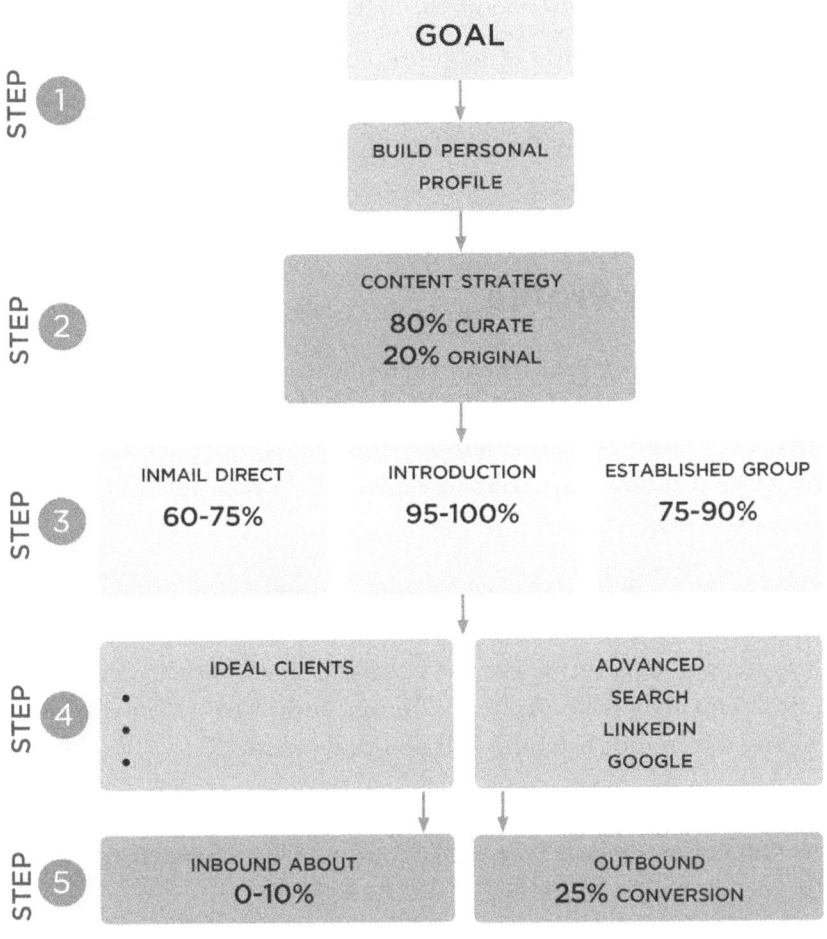

© Jane Anderson 2015

Step 1: Goal

What do you want to achieve with your profile? Do you want to get into a new market? Are you trying to find clients? Do you want to attract talent? Are you looking for strategic alliances? What is the purpose of your profile?

You can do all this work on your profile but if you're not clear about what you want, you're going to get frustrated because it's not working for you. What you're doing has to be crystal clear. To achieve that, you need to state who it is that you want to work with, what problems you solve and how you go about it.

Your profile is like a mirror. Your customer looks at your profile, thinking: "Where can I see me in your profile?" The unconscious decisions they make are about how you look – in keywords, in industries and the types of people you've worked with. It's far more about the customer and less about you. If it's all about you, you will ostracise people and repel them.

It was John F. Kennedy who said: "Efforts and courage are not enough without purpose and direction." You need to be clear about the niche you work with, your message and markets.

Step 1: Build Your Profile

Once you're clear about your goal, the next step is to focus on building your profile. The profile needs to be built around your goal and the future, not the past; otherwise, it will look like an obituary. This is often the step that is most overlooked and yet it is the most crucial, as you only have four seconds to help your reader understand what you do and how you help.

It's not all about you. There needs to be more emphasis on how you help your client, and less emphasis about what you love, what inspires you, or how you want to change the world. You need to make sure you use collateral that builds trust in your client and sings to the problems they have. As Matt Church, author of *Sell Your Thoughts*, says: "They don't care, they're not listening and you don't matter."

At this crucial stage, your profile needs to have full SEO so that you're turning up in search results and competing on keywords. Your profile also needs to be tested for the pages you are turning up on in LinkedIn and Google.

Step 2: Content Strategy

The next step involves looking at posting and content. You need to have a content strategy for what you're going to educate people about. About 80% of your content strategy should be sharing, commenting and liking content. The other 20% needs to be original content to educate people about your area of expertise.

This isn't necessarily about you selling stuff online. This is about how you address problems your customers have and what your thought leadership is in relation to that.

With the average person spending more than two hours per day on social media, you need to give them something to read. Robert Cialdini, the author of *Influence: the Psychology of Persuasion*, says that you need five to seven touch points to influence and persuade someone to do what you want them to do. Make content writing a habit and a priority – it is the number-one activity to be done each day or week, not something that is done when you have time.

Step 3: Connect

Clients we have worked with will say things such as: "I've tried doing direct approaches," or "I've tried doing introductions. I don't have any success," when they've only done one or two and given up. It's important you're clear about what is the benchmark.

Something that can really make a difference is this first-degree connection or the introduction. This is when you see someone's profile and you notice that they're connected to somebody you know, and you ask for an introduction, for example, "Would you mind?" or "Could you please connect me to ..." The key here is to manage how you're positioned when you're introduced. So you may like to write your introduction for them.

If you're in an established group that your ideal target person is also in, they're more likely to take notice of you. About 75-90% of people will be happy to connect with you that way, as long as the connection request is written correctly and you have written your own profile effectively. As the saying goes, "You only get one chance at a first impression!"

Step 4: Searches

You need to know where your market is and how to find it. Your market often includes busy people who aren't trying to find you, particularly if they don't know they have a problem. Sitting back and waiting for people to approach you will not get results.

Profiles of ideal clients can be found via various search functions in LinkedIn. The reality is that LinkedIn's search engine is not perfect and your ideal clients don't know how to optimise their profiles, or don't want to be found by you. This means you may have to use other means to find your ideal client on LinkedIn. It also means you need to think about the people you want to connect with and create customised conversations with. Using a spray-and-pray method only ostracises people and makes them feel like a commodity.

If you don't have a premium account, you won't have all the options of searching for all roles, but you will have some. A premium account will give you access to greater search functions and can be worth the investment if you are undertaking an aggressive growth strategy with your profile.

Step 5: Sales Meetings

The last step is knowing how to approach people and start a conversation. If you've been doing all your ground work, then you can start to have some scripts to use when talking to people.

If you're doing all the previous steps, about 90% of your leads on LinkedIn will want to meet with you. If you're getting in front of those people, you should be closing at least one in four sales and that's even if you're not a great salesperson. The remaining 10% of leads will come to you directly without you approaching them.

Reflections and Actions

- What is your goal with your profile? Are you looking for new clients, strategic partners, investors, etc.?
- Who do you help?
- What do you know that you can share with your connections?

Chapter 4

Search Engine Optimisation (SEO)

"The best place to hide a dead body is page 2 of Google search results."
— *Unknown*

Pull vs Push

Thomas Edison once said: "There's a better way to do it. Find it."

When Jane first started working with her mentor, she remembered thinking: "Where on Earth have you been for the past four years?!" She wished she had known he existed. She didn't know about him or his business.

He kept within his stream of clients but didn't do much social media marketing. For a Gen Y/X like Jane, that's where she hung out, so why did it take her so long to hear about him? She didn't find out about him until someone who was being mentored by him reached out to have a coffee with Jane to learn more about what she did. He told Jane about his mentor and she thought, "Wow, that's exactly what I'm after."

So, from a sales perspective, times have changed. We have moved into an era of the information superhighway. The challenge with this is that there is so much information available, unless you really know what you need, it can be hard to know where to turn. So you either procrastinate and do nothing, or buy what you think you need and then waste it. Cut-through is so important to connect with the right buyer for your business or for a recruiter.

Pull

In a pull strategy:

1. Someone needs help.
2. They ask around, do a Google search, and turn to their LinkedIn or Facebook connections.

3. They go to your website or LinkedIn profile.
   - They look at your photo and scan your title for keywords.
   - If you don't have them, they've gone.

This is relevant in a **network or search** and you require good search engine optimisation for your LinkedIn profile and website to get this to work.

In a strategy, you would typically do the following:

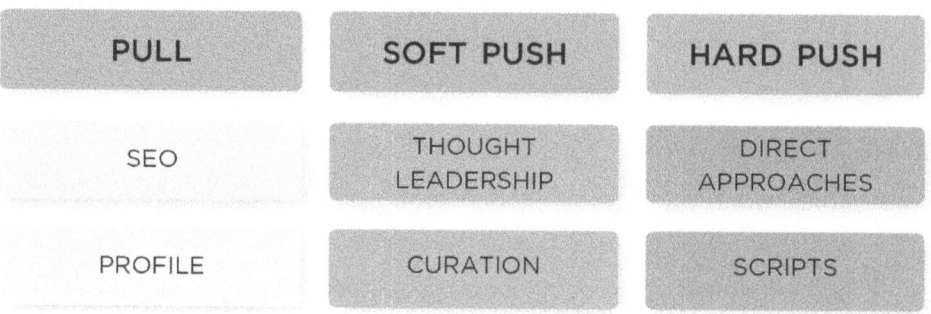

The main thing to keep in mind with Pull strategies is that you will still be validated. People will still find you online to check that you are who they've been told you are, if you know someone they know. So a Pull strategy is still very much part of the Push process.

Businesses need to leverage their teams' networks to build awareness of what they do to cover all angles. Accessibility, visibility and continuity are key.

Christopher Mahar from Motorola implemented a search engine optimisation strategy. He said: "Post your sessions and my new understanding of how to grow my profile and search engine optimisation, I have achieved the following LinkedIn success within one week.!"

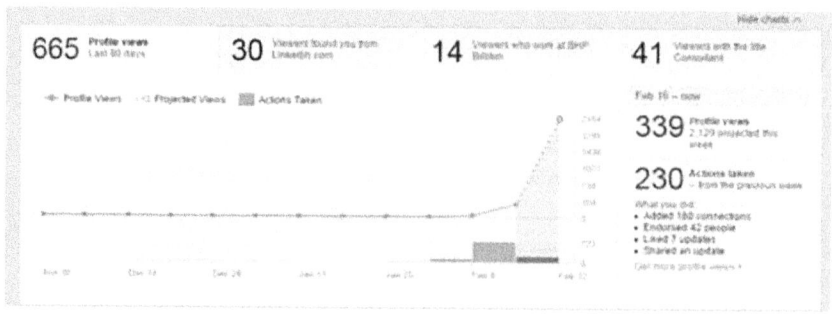

Get Found

Your LinkedIn profile generally has about four seconds to capture your readers' interest. An effective profile attracts your ideal audience.

Many people think LinkedIn is for job seekers, and although that is true, it is also a great low-cost tool for businesses to attract new clients. It can be a cost-effective strategy for consultants, small businesses and organisations.

By using LinkedIn effectively, you can be found in search results, position yourself as an expert in your field, and easily research prospective clients.

We recently spoke with a client who had a strong dislike for LinkedIn. He complained that the information he received wasn't relevant. After a quick search of his profile, we found that his LinkedIn profile had been written about his past, not his future. Writing about his past meant the LinkedIn search algorithm was providing him with information about exactly that. Remember that LinkedIn is about your future, so write your content to reflect this.

To support business-to-business sales, your LinkedIn profile needs to be found (search engine optimised) and needs to be marketable.

What Do You Want?

To deliver a strong LinkedIn strategy, it is important to first know what you want from LinkedIn. LinkedIn is not a mind reader and only understands data you enter. First and foremost, LinkedIn is an algorithm and a search engine.

It's a bit like a mirror and it will reflect what information you give it. The great news is that you can ask for what you want!

So, this leads to the question: "Who is your ideal audience?" With a clear picture of your audience, you will be able to communicate with them through your LinkedIn profile in a meaningful manner.

- What industry do they work in?
- What problems and challenges do they have?
- What are they most concerned about?
- Where do they congregate?
- Are they male or female?
- What age group might they be?

- What are their interests?
- What experience do you have working with them?
- Where do they eat?
- Where do they live?
- What do they do when they're not at work?
- What do they spend their time and money on?

When you're super clear about who you're talking to, then you can build a true connection with your audience and attract the opportunities you desire!

How Do You Know Where You're Turning Up in Search Results?

Sometimes, it can be hard to know if the work you put in to your profile is effective. Generally, we would expect to see increased engagement with your targeted audience and more leads.

There are a number of other measures of your LinkedIn profile's success. These include:

1. **Direct Google search results.**

You can do a direct search into Google (www.google.com). A well-optimised LinkedIn profile that includes a vanity URL will be returned in the search results.

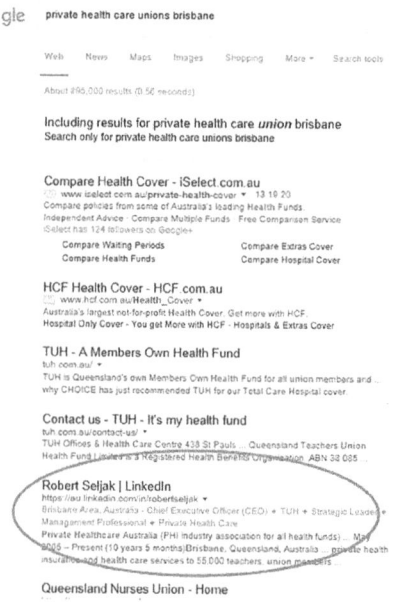

We have worked with clients where their LinkedIn profile is on the first page of the Google search terms. Of course, some keywords are more competitive than others. From an audience's perspective, these results are sometimes seen as more "authentic" than a company page on Google. Another advantage is that having your LinkedIn profile returned in search results is generally a cheaper option that paying for an SEO expert to keyword optimise your website.

For example, the initial results with SEO for a CEO in the health insurance industry had his LinkedIn profile returned on the first page of search results for the targeted keywords.

2. Search on LinkedIn directly and remove the parameters of connection. This option will also allow you to access others who appear in your results.

For example, if you are an accountant in Brisbane, you can put the words "accountant Brisbane" in the search box. This would be the same search a client would do.

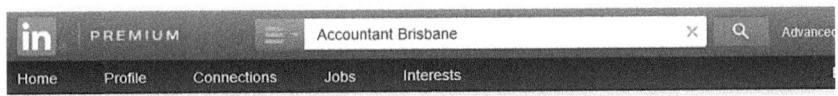

You can then see the right-hand side includes parameters that impact the search. These include:

1. People, Jobs, Companies, Groups, Universities, Posts and Inbox.
   Select People.
2. Relationship is the degree of connections. Select 3rd + Everybody else.
3. Select the location you want to search.

3. Perform a Google "X-ray" search for your client's keywords to check their rankings. Make sure you have logged out of your LinkedIn account. Enter the keyword into the Google browser.

site:linkedin.com/in | site:linkedin.com/pub -dir "Accountant" Brisbane
site:linkedin.com/in | site:linkedin.com/pub -inurl:pub/dir "Accountant" Brisbane

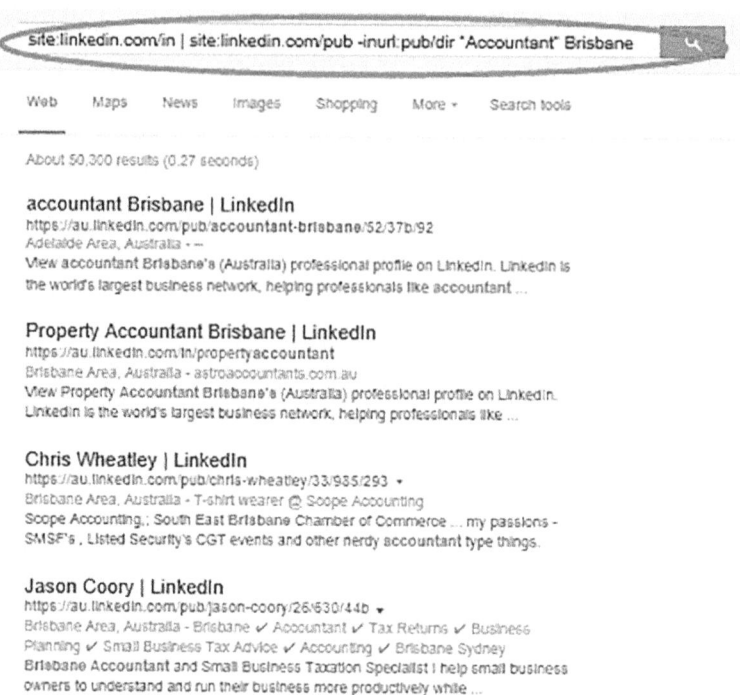

Having a fully search engine optimised LinkedIn profile – supported with blog posts, liking and commenting – directly and positively impacts Google and LinkedIn search results, meaning you have more visibility, more trust and more opportunities to work with your ideal audience.

Firstly, Be Found

It is vital to remember that **LinkedIn is a search engine**. This means it offers a great opportunity for you to be found by new clients. The key to this is SEO. LinkedIn is indexed heavily by Google.

Be Marketable

To support business-to-business selling, the profile needs to market yourself and your business, making it clear to the reader what is in it for them. A LinkedIn profile, for this purpose, needs to have a clear value proposition. What makes you different from others in your field?

The 5 Areas to Maximise Your LinkedIn SEO

The first and most important step with SEO is to identify and research keywords. Recently, we worked with a financial planner in Brisbane, Australia. This client specialised in retirement planning in Brisbane.

We thought about his ideal clients and words they would use to find people like him. We considered words such as "financial planning", "retirement planning" and "Brisbane". Think about who you want to be found by and what words they would use. You need to build your profile around keywords your ideal audience would use – not industry-specific buzz words. Not sure what words your ideal audience would use? You can always ask them what words they use when doing a Google search.

Once you have your keywords, conduct your own search on these words and see what people are returned in the search results. Is it what you expected? Once you have identified your keywords and have done some research, you can build your content and profile around these words.

LinkedIn has never shared its algorithm. However, based on research, you need to fully search engine optimise your profile. By not ensuring that you have the correct keywords, not only will you not be found, but you won't attract your ideal client because you won't make sense to them in less than four seconds. So your profile's a bit like a magnet: you will either repel or attract your ideal client or audience.

Think about what people you want to find you and what words they would use. Once you have identified your keywords, you can build your content around them.

There are five areas that will fully search engine optimise your profile. These include your:

1. **Title:** You have 120 characters to work with for your title and it needs to reflect your keywords and the problems your customer has.

2. **Summary:** The summary is a key component of your LinkedIn profile. The summary positions you for your target audience. It offers a great opportunity to include keywords, validation and a strong call to action.

3. **Employment history:** You can use up to 2000 characters for each position you've held in this space. Essentially, this is your positioning area and it needs to reflect your customers' problems, why should they care, how you can help, who trusts you, and leverage testimonials.

4. **Skills and endorsements:** You might be endorsed for things you've never

heard of before or by people you've never met, but these still carry a heavy weighting in the search results, so you can take control of them. You don't need to accept what people give you and you don't need to prioritise the numbers on your profile that LinkedIn gives you. You have complete control over it.

5. **Recommendations:** You might need to help people write recommendations for you, but they are a high priority on your profile.

Blog posts also contribute to search engine optimisation, as well as being returned in search results with your name, headshot and headline.

Other character limitations include:

- **Website label:** 30 maximum characters.
- **Website URL:** 256 maximum characters.
- **Company name:** 100 maximum characters.
- **Job title:** 100 maximum characters.

Keywords are based on your goals moving forward and may not directly reflect what you are doing at the moment. For example, we worked with a member-based organisation that had a reputation for servicing teachers, and was looking to expand into other industries, such as nursing. In this instance, the profile was developed around attracting nurses and other future clients industries, as well as teachers.

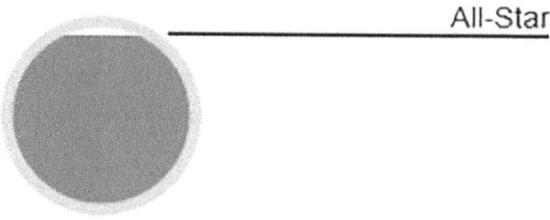

You can also use Google AdWords' Keyword Tool to figure out which terms will increase your searchability. **Keyword Planner** is a free **AdWords** tool that finds **keyword** ideas and estimates how they may perform in Google searches. Although it is for Google and not LinkedIn, you will get an idea of words being used. To access Google Keyword Planner, you need to set up an AdWords account. You can find out more here: https://adwords.google.com/KeywordPlanner

Action Steps to Get Started

Go to htttps://www.linkedin.com/

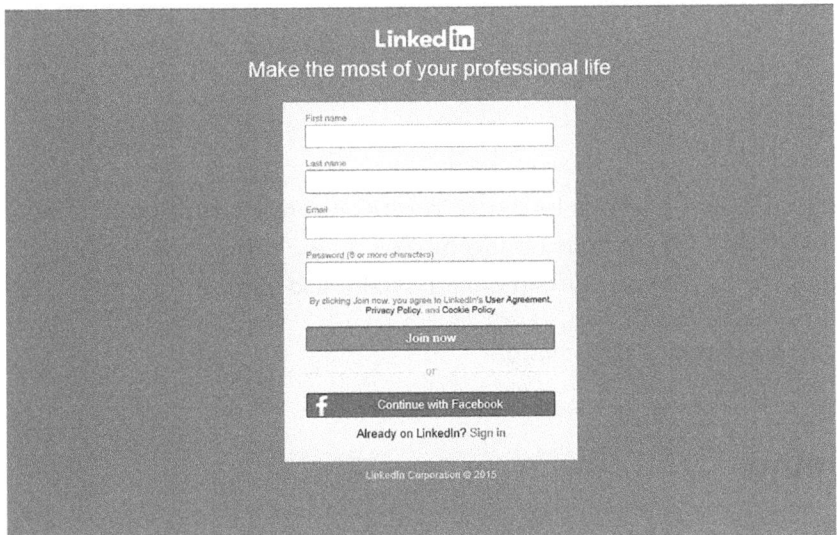

1. Fill in all the details and click "Join Now".
2. You will receive an email confirmation that you need to accept so you can get started.

The Title (Headline)

The headline looks like this:

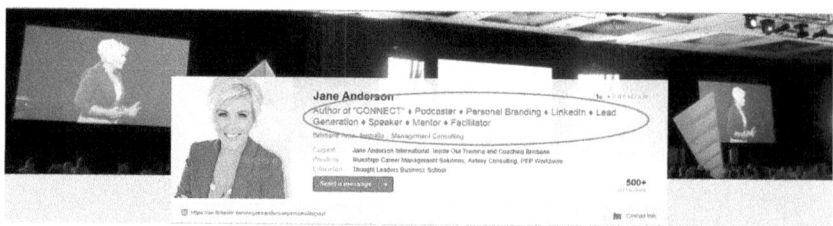

Kylie Chown

Reach Certified LinkedIn Strategist & Master Resume Writer | Crafting Profiles and Resumes that Elevate High Performers

Brisbane Area, Australia | Writing and Editing

The title or headline of your LinkedIn profile sits under your name. The default setting on LinkedIn will set your title to be exactly the same as your current role. Most of the clients we see make a fundamental mistake and leave it that way.

Why is this so important to change?

Positioning

Without the correct heading, you will be pigeonholed into the category people think you belong to, rather than perceived how you want to be. For example, if you have "CEO of Pegasus Pty Ltd", that doesn't tell me how you help me. I have to do a lot more reading to find out and, frankly, I don't have time. As Rachel Bourke, a leading expert in sales, says in her book The YES Zone: "A confused mind says 'no'." So if it's not clear to your reader how you can help them, your ideal client will pigeonhole you as a CEO who can't help them, when in fact you can. You just haven't sold it early enough in your profile.

Validation

Firstly, when your profile is returned in search results, the name, headline and photo will be the only sections of your profile that are visible. This means that the photo, headline and name are the determining factors for whether somebody is going to click through to your profile. It is imperative you use your title as a positioning statement for how you want to be found. When somebody is viewing your profile in search results, you only have three to four seconds to make an impact. The best way to do this is with a standout headline.

Search Engine Optimisation

Your title contributes to your search engine optimisation, so include keywords where possible. You have 120 characters in the headline to maximise your findability.

A well-written title distinguishes you from people with similar skills and expertise. If your keywords include a target location, you can include this in your headline as well.

Getting Click Through

Once you have keyword optimisation, you can apply the "who you are and who you help" principle.

Here are some great examples of headlines:

- Executive Gemologist serving CEOs. Cut, Polishing and Resetting the Inner Diamonds of Executives and their Companies.
- Business Development Co-ordinator ♦ Health Insurance ♦ Enhancing the Customer Experience for Teachers and Union Members.
- Environmental Leadership ♦ Project Manager ♦ Oil & Gas, Perth ♦ Positively Impacting the Environment, Safety and People.
- Specialist Technical Trainer Providing WH&S, Rehabilitation and Return-to-Work Services to the Health Insurance Sector.
- Industrial Relations (IR) Specialist – Driving Major IR Projects in the Australian Oil, Gas and Iron Ore Sectors.
- CEO | Company Name | Partnering with Business on Customised Solutions to Effortlessly Achieve Project Excellence.

We have worked with clients to create multiple headlines, and then tested them on a rotational basis to see what achieves the best click-through. You can do this to see what gets you the best results.

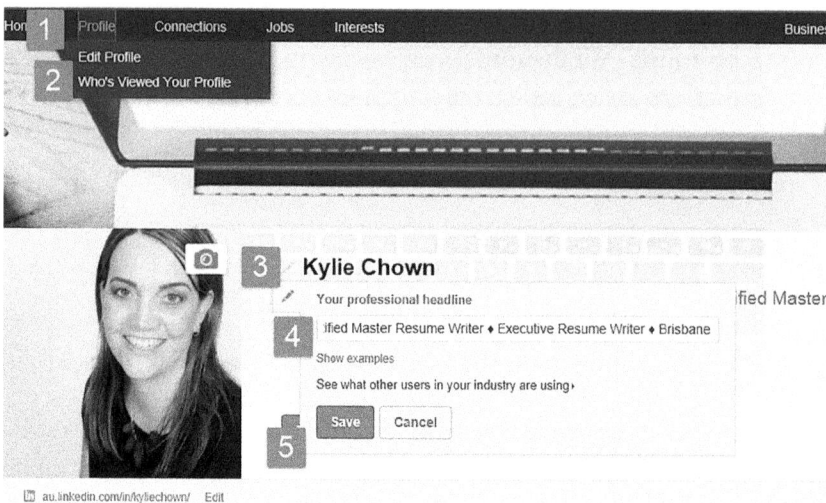

Action Steps to Create Your Stand-Out Title

1. Click Profile.
2. Click Edit Profile.
3. Click
4. Write your new headline.
5. Click Save
6. Do a search and you will be able to see how your profile is returned in search results.

Top Tip #1: Use typology symbols (♦□❖●) to break use words, increase readability and minimise conjoint words.

Top Tip #2: If the location is part of your SEO strategy, use it in your headline.

Summary

We live in a competitive world and if you want to make an impact, you need to be in control of your online presence, personal brand, cultural fit and reputation.

Here is what a summary looks like:

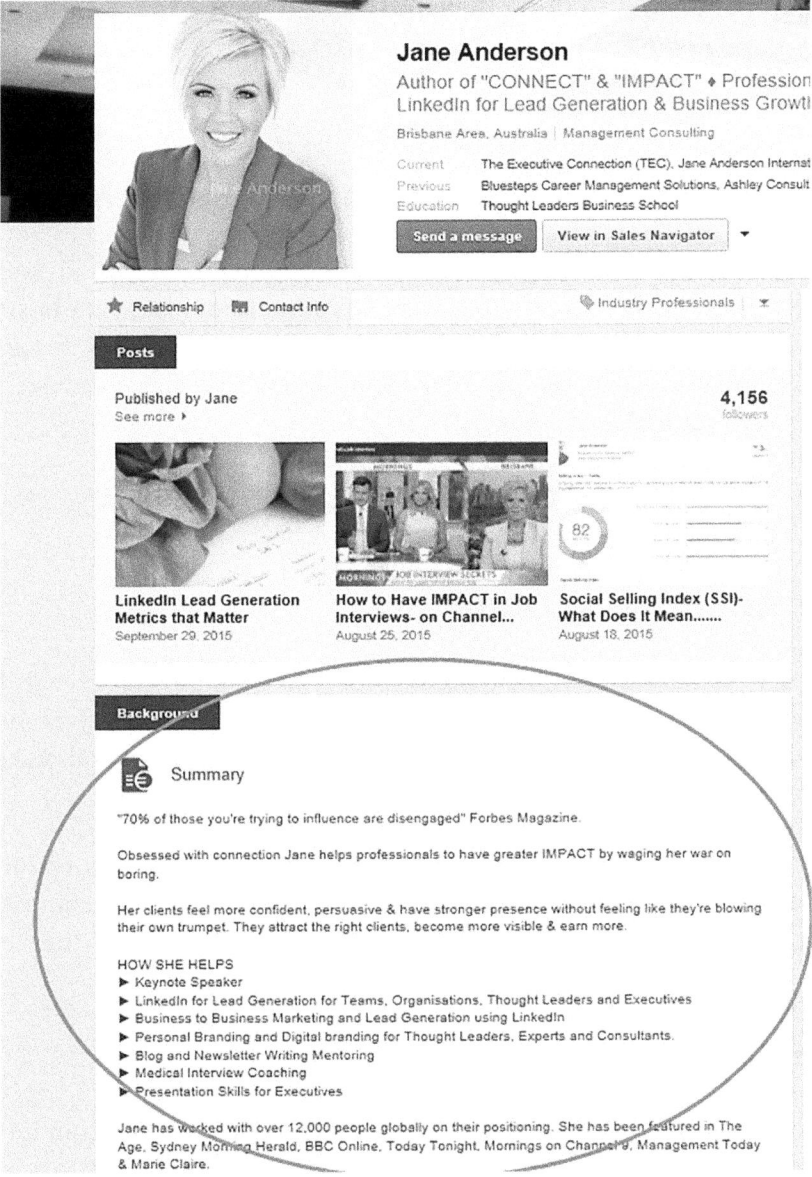

Failing to give adequate attention to your LinkedIn profile may not only result in you missing out on potential contacts; you also run the risk of trailing behind your competitors.

In Ctrl Alt Delete, Mitch Joel introduces "digital first": the concept that the first place we learn about people is online. This means that people are making decisions based on what they read online, so you don't even know the opportunities you could be missing.

Understand people are making decisions based on the information they read. It is potentially the first place people find information on you and decide whether to take further action.

Importance of the LinkedIn Summary Section

Many people don't realise the importance of a great summary section in your LinkedIn profile. More than any other section, the summary represents you, your business and your brand. It is also the most viewed section on LinkedIn. If you get this area right, you are well on the way to having one of the most viewed profiles on LinkedIn – and attracting more of your target audience.

Here are a few top tips for creating a successful LinkedIn summary:

Be Clear About Your Objective

Before writing your summary, be clear about what you want to achieve with LinkedIn. Are you using it to raise your credibility or are you looking to expand your network? Are you seeking new clients? Understand what you are trying to do and make sure this is clear in your summary.

The key to a strong LinkedIn summary is writing for your future, not your past. You need to make it relevant to your audience. Make a strong, compelling summary that will have your ideal audience thinking you are what they need to solve their problem

LinkedIn Summary

Your summary meets the blend of keywords and your purpose. The content will be targeted to your audience and purpose. For a job seeker, think about content that will engage a recruiter. For a sales professional, think about your clients. If you are a thought leader, how can you demonstrate your expertise? This section is limited to only 2000 characters, so we recommend the following layout:

1st Paragraph:

This is your LinkedIn elevator speech. If I read the first sentence only, I have a strong sense of you and your offerings. These tasks need to match the keywords you want to be found with. For example:

"I am a professional leadership coach with more than 15 years of experience in leadership, consulting, human resources and performance management. Tertiary qualified with a wide variety of local and international experience."

2nd paragraph:

The next paragraph can highlight your core focus areas. These include specialist skills that relate to keywords. Include what you want to be known for and what makes you different from others like you. For example:

"I help executives in the finance industry gain clarity and direction. My core focus areas include: executive coaching, behavioural-based recruitment and performance management."

3rd paragraph:

Now you need to support your skills with evidence. How have you assisted your clients? What issues have you resolved? Have you increased engagement or efficiency? What have others said? Have you won any awards? For example:

"Achievements include ..." and list your top three to five achievements.

"After working with me, what some have said includes ..."

4th paragraph:

This is a great spot to introduce your role within your current organisation and leverage any internal marketing communications. At this point, you are elevating your capacity to be a brand ambassador. If you are a job seeker, you can leverage brands you have worked for. For example:

"I am the business development manager for ABC Company. At ABC Company, we help the mining sector to minimise costs and project delivery time frames."

Finally, we need a strong call to action, a "where to from here?" For example:

"To see how we can help your team reduce costs, email me at ..."

"Ready to commit to my next opportunity, you can contact me at ..."

Ensure your LinkedIn summary aligns with who you are. It isn't about what you have done or how successful you have been. The words in your summary are about making an emotional connection with the reader. The best way to do this is by using emotive language and keywords. Recent research shows that people will decide whether to contact you within a few seconds of reading your profile.

Action Steps to Create a Stand-Out Summary

To edit your summary, log into your LinkedIn profile and:

1. Click Profile.
2. Edit Profile.

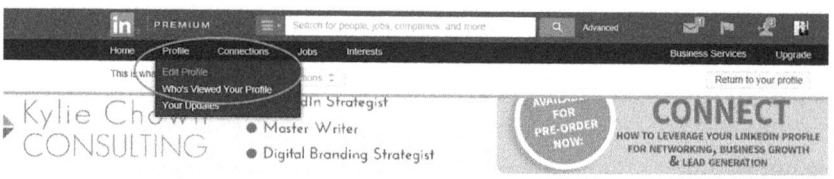

3. Scroll to the summary section.

4. Write your summary.
5. Click Save

Top Tip #1: Make it easy for people to contact you. Having a strong call to action that includes contact details means prospective clients can easily take further action.

Top Tip #2: Most people aren't aware that they can find your contact information on other people's profiles.

Skills, Expertise and Endorsements

Many clients ask why they should bother with skills, expertise and endorsements. Skills, expertise and endorsements on LinkedIn give a clear and immediate picture of your abilities. Your endorsements also contribute to your SEO, as well as influencing those who look at your profile.

Kylie recently spoke to a client who was an accountant and had recently bought a new home. He noticed that his real estate agent had endorsed him for financial planning skills. The accountant was perplexed – why was his real estate agent endorsing him for a skill he knew nothing about?

This will often happen because the default setting on LinkedIn makes suggestions to your contacts on what they should endorse you for. There is the option to manually over-ride this setting so that your skills are not suggested endorsements for others.

On your profile, your skills and endorsements look like this:

Control What You Are Endorsed For and How This is Presented on Your Profile

Although we can't control who is endorsing us, we can control what we are endorsed for, the order they appear and their visibility within your profile.

The first step to having quality endorsements is controlling what you are endorsed for. The easiest way to do that is to manually add skills and expertise to your profile. We recommend that clients look at their endorsements and re-order or even hide endorsements so that they are reflective of their current goals and objectives.

LinkedIn provides you with the capacity to include up to 50 skills. Our advice when starting out is to only include your strongest skills. It is better to have 10 strong skills than 50 possible options diluting your endorsements. Once you have built these results, you can add more skills to your profile.

Leverage Endorsements

Having worked with thousands of profiles, we have found that recommendations are weighted more heavily than endorsements. If you want to increase the testimonials in your LinkedIn profile, you can start by looking at who has endorsed you. You already know these people think highly of your work and are prepared to say so in a public space, so you may consider asking them for a testimonial.

Endorsements for Others

By endorsing others, you will increase your own viability when that person is viewed in LinkedIn, but remember that what you endorse others for also reflects on you. Only first-level connections can endorse you, so by growing your network you are growing your possible endorsers. It also helps others to understand what you're known for.

Top Tip: List skills that are consistent with future industry needs to be ahead of the game. For example, if there is imminent change for your industry, list this as a skill. This gives you the opportunity to be endorsed for it and supports search engine optimisation outcomes.

Action Steps to Manage Skills, Experience and Endorsements

Once you have logged into your profile:

1. Click Profile.
2. Click Edit Profile.

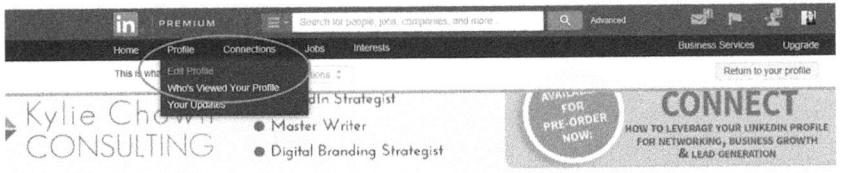

3. Scroll to Skills and Endorsements. Under the Skills and Endorsements setting, personalise the check boxes.

This will take you to the next screen.

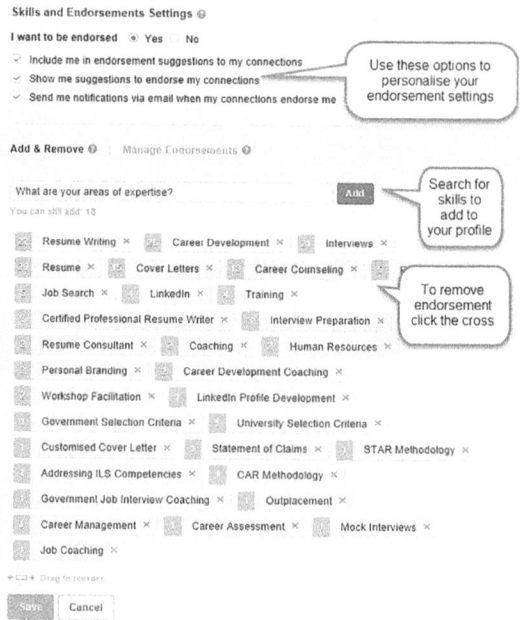

4. Add skills and expertise by typing in skills.

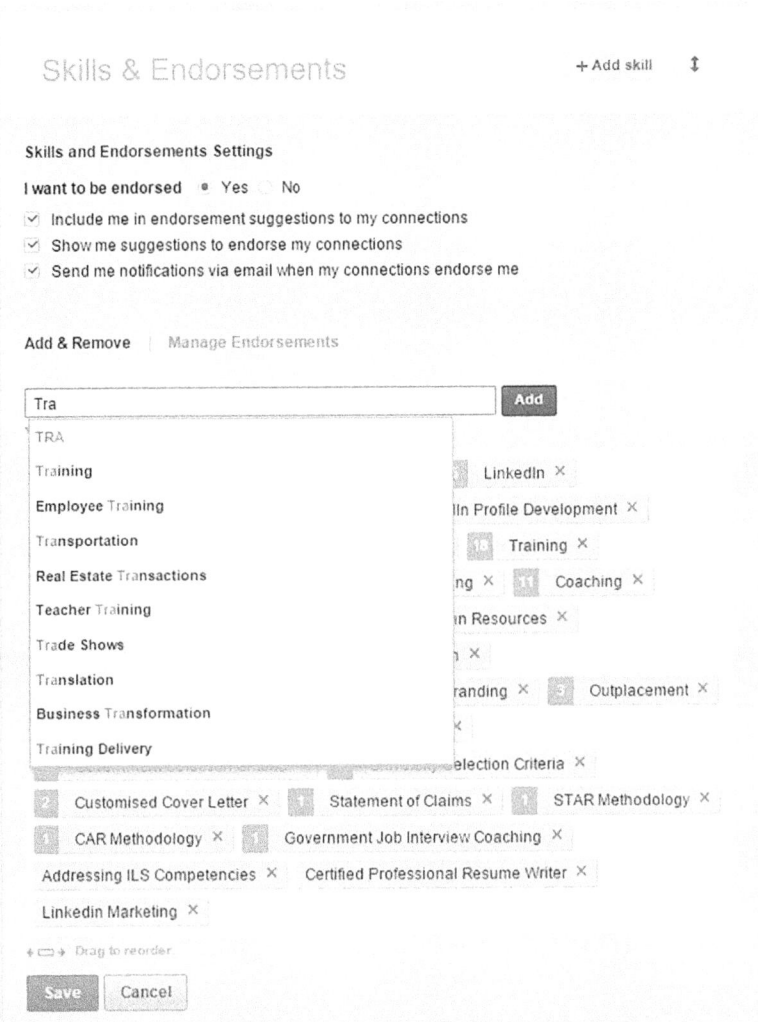

5. To remove endorsements, click the cross.

6. Click Save

Top Tip: If you are endorsed by someone, it is a good idea to send them a quick thank you note. If you are endorsed by someone, you don't need to endorse them in return, especially if you are not confident of their skill set.

Employment History

We often say to our clients, **"Your LinkedIn is all about your future and not your past,"** and this is especially true for your employment history.

Your employment history is not an obituary of your past jobs; it is a search engine optimised sales and marketing tool!

By taking this approach to your LinkedIn profile, you will be able to leverage its social selling capabilities to your advantage.

A fully completed employment entry looks like this:

 Experience

LinkedIn Profile Writer for Business & Job Seekers | Master Resume Writer | Executive Resume Writer
Kylie Chown Consulting Services
February 2014 – Present (1 year 9 months) | Australia Wide (Brisbane, Sydney, Melbourne)

Offering assured solutions and purposeful results, I am inspired on a daily basis to see my clients elevate their on and offline presence, increase their business outcomes and take their career to the next level. I work with businesses and individuals across a range of industries.

CORE FOCUS AREAS:
⇢ Executive Resume Writer.
⇢ LinkedIn Profile Optimisation - Thought Leaders, Executives and Managers.
⇢ LinkedIn Profile Optimisation - Business Development Teams, Small Business Owners, Solopreners and Consultants.
⇢ LinkedIn Profile Optimisation - Professional Jobseekers.

FEATURED IN:
⇢ Australian Institute of Management (AIM)
⇢ Minnovare Mining and Civil
⇢ Franchise Business
⇢ Leaders In Heels
⇢ HC and HRM Online
⇢ Women in Leadership and Management Australasia (WILMA)
⇢ Guest Speaker for the Electus Recruitment Seminar for Job Seekers

CREDENTIALS:
♦ Reach Certified Branding Analyst (1 of 3 Australia Wide)
♦ Certified Master Résumé Writer (1 of 8 Australia Wide)
♦ Certified Executive Resume Master (1 of 4 Australia Wide)
♦ Certified Resume Specialist (Sales and Business Development)
♦ Certified Advanced Résumé Writer
♦ Certified Professional Online Job Search and Reputation Management

Some feedback I have received is:

"I really like how you converted my very technical resume into a more user friendly document without losing any of the content" IT Manager, VIC.

It is important to remember that your LinkedIn profile **isn't written for you – you are writing for your audience.** Make sure the information in the Employment History is clear, well organised and easy to read.

It is also important to remember that your LinkedIn profile is a public document that anyone can potentially view. You need to be mindful of the information you place in your profile.

A great formula to follow when writing your employment history is **ISCR (Introduction, Specialties, Company and Results).**

Top Tip: Keep in mind what your audience's problems are and write about how you solve them.

The Introduction

This is a brief overview of what you did in the position, who you engaged with and for what reason. As an example: "As the business development manager for ABC Company, I provided expert advice, guidance and recommendations for a range of products that include …"

If the reader was to only read the first line of your employment history, they should have a clear idea of your job and what you did in that role. You need to capture your job in a single sentence.

Here are some other examples:

"As the senior IT systems manager for ABC Company, I provide team leadership and operational management to the Brisbane-based team."

"As the account manager for ABC Company, I developed and supported customers to navigate the superannuation maze."

"As the sales manager, I led a team while managing high-value accounts within the ABC business."

These examples show that in just one sentence, you get a strong idea of what these people did in their roles.

The Specialties

In this area, you can highlight your main competencies. The key here is to align the competencies with SEO. Here is an example of how to present your specialties:

My specialties at ABC Company include:

- ◆ *Relationship Management*
- ◆ *Account Management*
- ◆ *Business Development*

Some other examples of specialties include:

- Stakeholder Engagement
- Financial Planning
- Team Leadership
- Coaching and Mentoring
- Board Reporting
- Strategic Planning

The Company

This is a great opportunity to leverage your internal marketing and communications functions to further validate your profile. You can utilise the confidence your client has in your brand to further elevate your profile.

Review the company website and pick key information that supports your branding. Anything that includes facts and figures will be well received. How many customers does the company have? What is the company's main achievements? Has it won any awards? Think about this from your client's point of view. What information would be important to them?

As an example:

"At ABC Company, we have more than 5,000 business customers who rely on us to provide critical services. As a leader in the field, we were recently nominated for the 2014 Business of the Year Award."

The Result

The result is your time to shine. Think about achievements your ideal audience will value as opposed to what you value. Recently, we worked with a client who was targeting an organisation that had a strong focus on customer service. For this reason, we decided to include achievements that supported this company's values. We went with something like:

"During this time I have:

- *Achieved a 5-Star Customer Service rating directly reflective of my service-driven approach.*
- *Solved all customer problems at the first point of call, mitigating the requirement for escalation."*

Results can be further supported by testimonials. For example:

What others have said after working with me includes:

"Robert is a customer-focused business development manager. Before Robert, any problems were processed in the call centre. Now Robert personally manages to resolve all issues directly. This means our business can do what we do best."

If the people who have provided a testimonial are happy to include their name, you can do so. You can also include the location. This works particularly well if you are targeting a particular location.

Finally, have a strong call to action. At this point, you have been found in search results. Your reader has read through and now needs a clear directive on where to go next. For example:

"To see how I can help you and your team, email me at (include email) or phone (include phone number)."

There is a limit of 2,000 characters per role within the employment section. If you have trouble deciding what to include, always revert back to your audience. Ask yourself, "Is this important to them?"

Action Steps to Adding Your Employment History

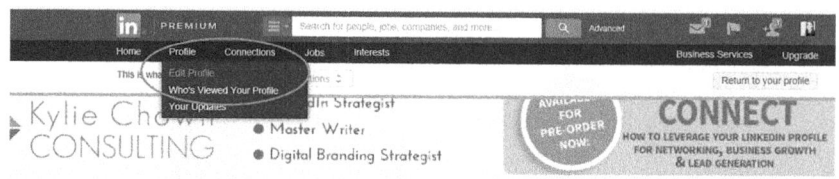

1. Under the Experience section, click +Add Position.

2. Start writing the name of the company you work for in the Company Name section. If the company is listed in LinkedIn, you can select it from the list. If not, you will need to add a new company.

3. You can then add in the fields of Title (what your current job title is), Location (where this role is situated) and the Time Period that you have worked at the company.

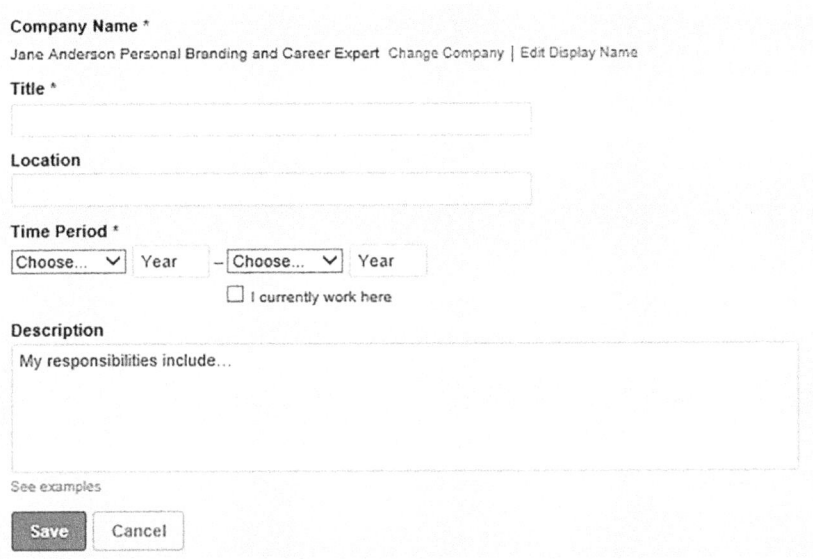

4. Under the Description, you can use the ISCR formula to complete the description of the role.

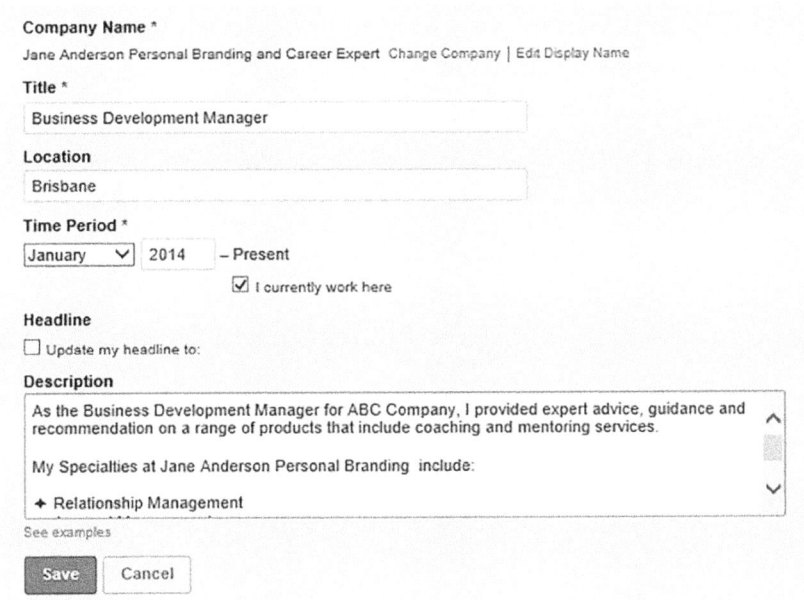

Important Pointer

The default setting is **Update my headline** to: Box checked. You need to uncheck this box.

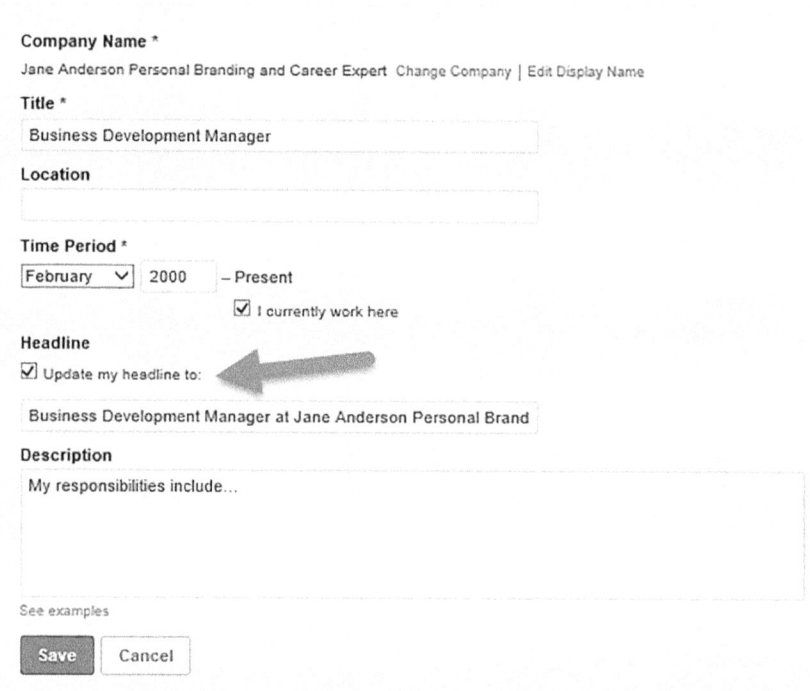

Top Tip: With 2,000 characters per role, your employment history is key to leveraging full search engine optimisation outcomes.

Publications

The Publications section lets you connect external content that you have authored or published to your profile.

Publications looks like this:

Publications

IMPACT: How to Build Your Personal Brand for the Connection Economy
Jane Anderson
October 1, 2014

Discover how to create 'corporation you' without being a tall poppy

We're no longer in the industrial or information age. We're now in the connection economy. The economy where you're ability to stand out, connect with others and position yourself in your career and business mean security. It means you won't be left behind but instead ahead of the pack.

Understanding Y
Wiley
May 18, 2014

Understanding Y is a fresh and incisive book that offers a better understanding, appreciation and awareness of the Millennial generation. In this groundbreaking work, author Charlie Caruso has amassed a diverse array of papers, articles and journals from prominent individuals, noted entrepreneurs and bestselling authors who collectively explore how Gen Y thinks, interacts and works. Understanding... more

▸ 7 authors, including:

 Jane Anderson
Author of "CONNECT" & "IMPACT" ♦ Pr...

 Charlie Caruso
Communications Entrepreneur

Chris Piper

Bernard Salt

Should You Lie About Being Fired?
The Age
March 25, 2014

Ever suffered the frustration and humiliation of being fired? Then you'll know the dilemma of deciding whether to be honest with prospective employers.

How to Stand Out With Your LinkedIn Summary
Leaders in Heels
August 26, 2013

Many people don't realise the importance of a great summary section in your LinkedIn profile. More than any other section, this area, represents you, your business and your brand. It is also the most viewed section on LinkedIn. If you get this area right, you are well on the way to having one of the most viewed profiles on LinkedIn – and attracting more of your target audience.

This is particularly useful if you have had your work published on other mediums. It also reduces any issues with posts being duplicated on other sites and Google penalising you.

Publications supports thought leadership and establishes your expert status. If you have contributed to an article, you can show this collaboration in the Publications section.

Top Tip: If you have been featured on another site, you can use Publications to highlight this.

Action Steps to Add a Publication

After Profile, go to Edit Profile.

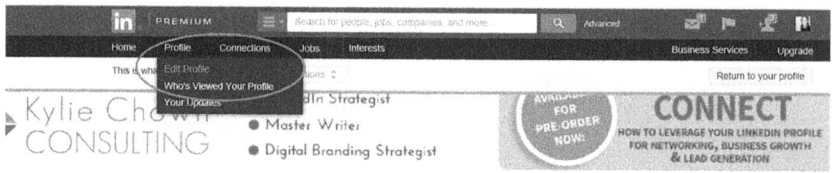

Scroll to Publications.

1. Enter the **Title** of the Publication.
2. Enter the **Publication or Publisher**.
3. Enter the **Date**.
4. Enter the **Publication URL**. You can use this field if you have been published on another site.
5. Your profile will be automatically added as an Author. You can add a co-author by typing their names.
6. In the **Description**, write a summary of your publication.
7. Click **Save**

It is important that publications don't sell a product or service. For thought leadership to be effective, publications need to be about educating and informing.

Plugins

Plugins offer a great opportunity to support and leverage internal communication and marketing functions. You can review your organisation's marketing collateral to include links in your own profile. LinkedIn allows you to add different types of media to your profile as a plugin. You can include:

- PowerPoint presentations
- Websites
- Videos
- PDF files
- YouTube channels

You can add plugins to three sections of your profile. These are:

- Summary
- Experience
- Education

Some ways that you can use plugins to support social selling include:

- Company advertising campaigns
- Customer testimonials
- Product and service information and education
- Contact Us page
- Speaker show reels

Jane's plugins look like this:

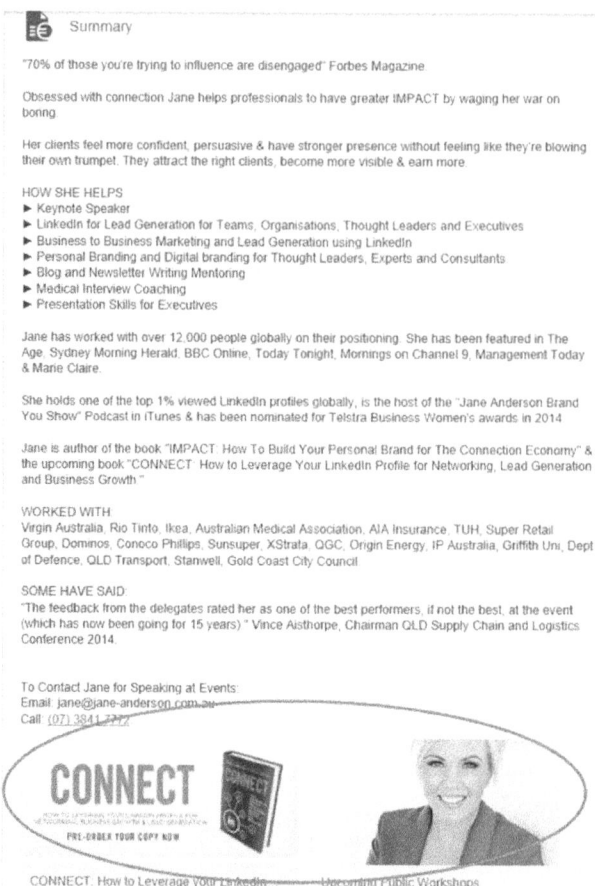

By adding company plugins to your profile, you can maintain the individualisation of your own profile while leveraging your organisation's marketing strategies. You can add plugins to websites or files.

To Add a Plugin Website

1. Under Profile, go to Edit Profile.

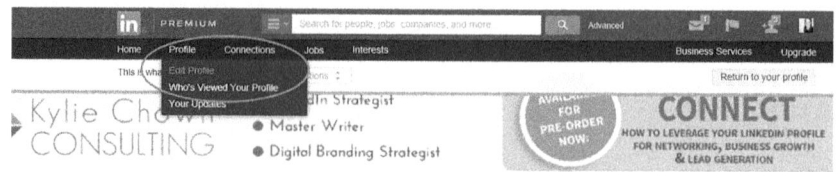

2. Go to Edit Summary, then Add Link or Upload File.

3. Type the address of the site you would like to add.

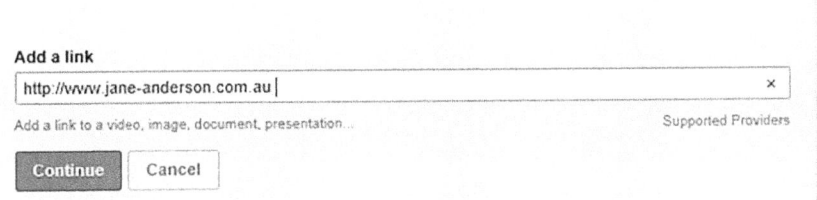

4. Once you select continue, the content will link to your profile. You can edit the description and add to the profile.

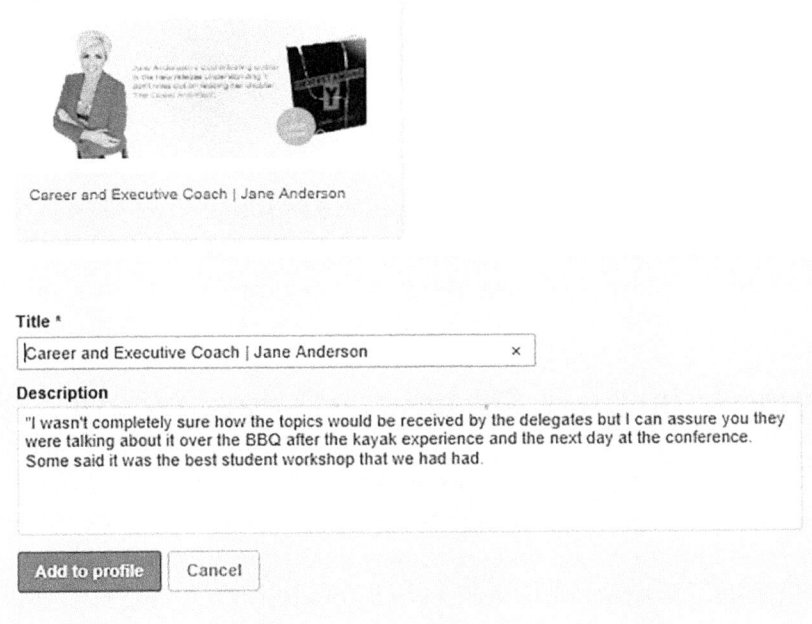

How to Add a File to Publications

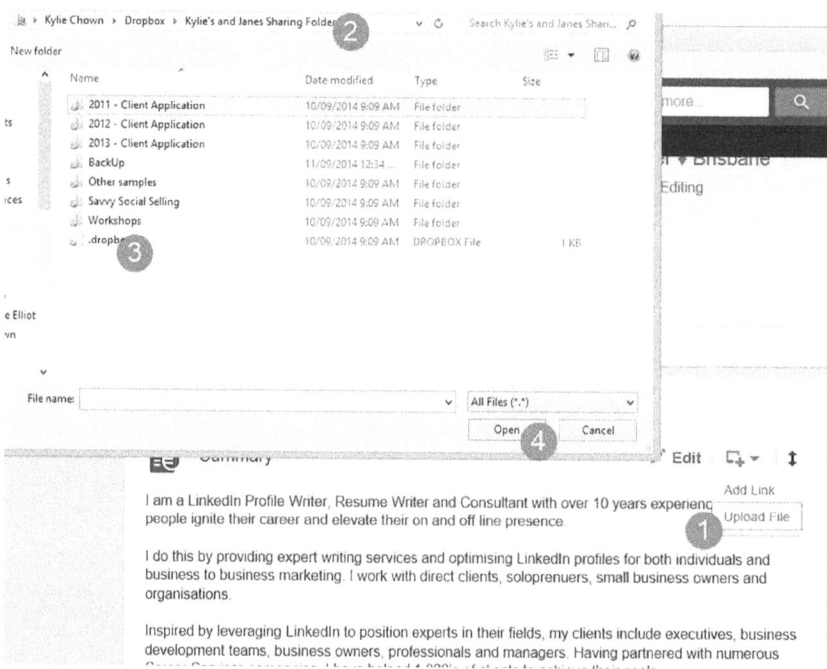

1. Click Add Link and Upload File.
2. Locate the directory.
3. Select the file.
4. Open the file.
5. Click Save

Top Tip: You can overwrite the content and descriptions from what is pulled from LinkedIn. By overwriting the content, you can further engage your audience. For example: "To find out more about our services, click here to view our website."

Testimonials and Recommendations

We recently worked with a group of salespeople to build their personal brand as thought leaders in their industry. We spent a considerable amount of time talking about testimonials and their value. Testimonials (or Recommendations) are what is called "social proof". When a potential client is looking at working with you, they need to see if someone else has said that you are good too work with.

Like a business, we have something to sell or something we want to create an influence with. So what's the benefit of testimonials for your target audience?

1. **They give hope:** The person looking at your testimonials uses their imagination to think, "Wow, I would love that to happen for me." They make the direct connection between what they need and how you can help them without you telling them.

2. **What others say about us is more important than what we say about ourselves:** Quite often, we work with clients to tone back their self-selling and let others do the talking.

3. **Brand leverage:** If that person has a position or works for a well-recognised brand, they will make a decision to call you based on brand association. This will give them confidence about who you have worked with before. It sends a clear message about who you CAN help.

4. **The potential client sees themselves in the client you have helped:** Based on stereotype, the potential client will make their own connection about your client and they'll think, "They're just like me," "That's exactly the problem I'm having," or "That's exactly the result I want."

5. **It's easier:** You don't need to write a truckload of content to sell yourself; recommendations and testimonials will do the majority of the work for you. By the time you get to a client meeting, you'll be answering the question, "When can you begin helping us?" rather than spending the meeting proving yourself.

Explore different ways you can make it easier for your potential clients or recruiters to see what others have to say about you on your website or LinkedIn profile. Making them dig will only let your competition beat you to the post. Here are some examples:

Professional Speaker, Author, Mentor on IMPACT
Jane Anderson International

Melissa Groom
CEO at Empowered Mums/Video Marketing Specialist/Host of Mums In Business TV

" Jane Anderson is a wealth of knowledge when it comes to branding and standing out in the market place. She is very professional, warm, friendly and a funny young lady with a real genuineness for wanting to help others.

Her presentation was very interactive and engaging and our members gained a lot of knowledge from her talk.

I would highly recommend Jane as a... more

August 6, 2015, Melissa was a consultant or contractor to Jane at Jane Anderson International

Jon Lindsay
Mentor for Business Leaders; Facilitator of Joined Up Thinking for Executive Teams

" Jane spoke last week to my two TEC groups on the subject "LinkedIn for CEO's, what's the benefit?" Since I have a few healthy sceptics in the groups we were conscious we weren't necessarily speaking to the converted. Jane came across as a true professional and of the greatest importance she was very aware of the nature of the group she was speaking to.
Because of her... more

June 21, 2015, Jon was a consultant or contractor to Jane at Jane Anderson International

Karin Flemm
Program, Project, Administration Manager ♦ Change Manager ♦ Process Improvement ♦ Consultant ♦ Writer ♦ Trainer

" I recently heard Jane speak at the Origin Energy WELL group, and her presentation about how to have IMPACT in today's online-dominated job search environment immediately changed my entire approach to my current search for a new opportunity. Her genuine desire to help people achieve their professional aspirations impressed me profoundly, as did her generosity with... more

June 7, 2015, Karin was Jane's client

A good testimonial includes a before and after. For example, "Before working with this person, I ..." (This brings up the known unspoken of your potential customer. This means that the potential customer can relate to the person giving the testimonial.) "After working with them, I now ..."

Here is an example from Kylie's profile:

LinkedIn Profile Writer | LinkedIn Strategist | LinkedIn for Business | LinkedIn for Job Seekers
Kylie Chown Consulting

Jade Hedley
Director, BE social. BE savvy. Brand, Graphic Design, Web, Marketing Campaigns for Small / Medium Business

" Before meeting Kylie I was unsure as to whether I required a presence on LinkedIn. I stuck in my comfort zone; Facebook. But since joining I've made many connections and it's been great for my business. It's resulted new clients and has led me to discover that my ideal client (target market) is in fact on LinkedIn. I have had comments made about the professionalism of my bio, yet it still depicts my personality. The training Kylie provided was fantastic so I felt confident to jump straight on and engage with people. **less**

June 6, 2015, Jade was Kylie's client

Action Steps to Manage Testimonials

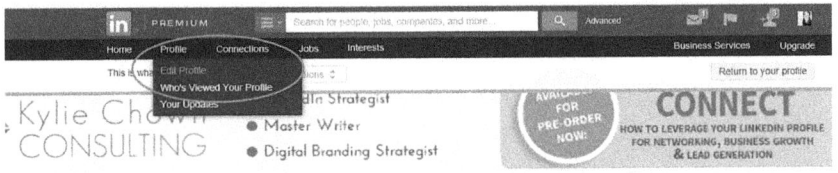

1. Under Recommendations, click Manage.

There are four sections: Received, Given, Ask for Recommendations and Give Recommendations.

1. Under Received:

You can view all your received recommendations.

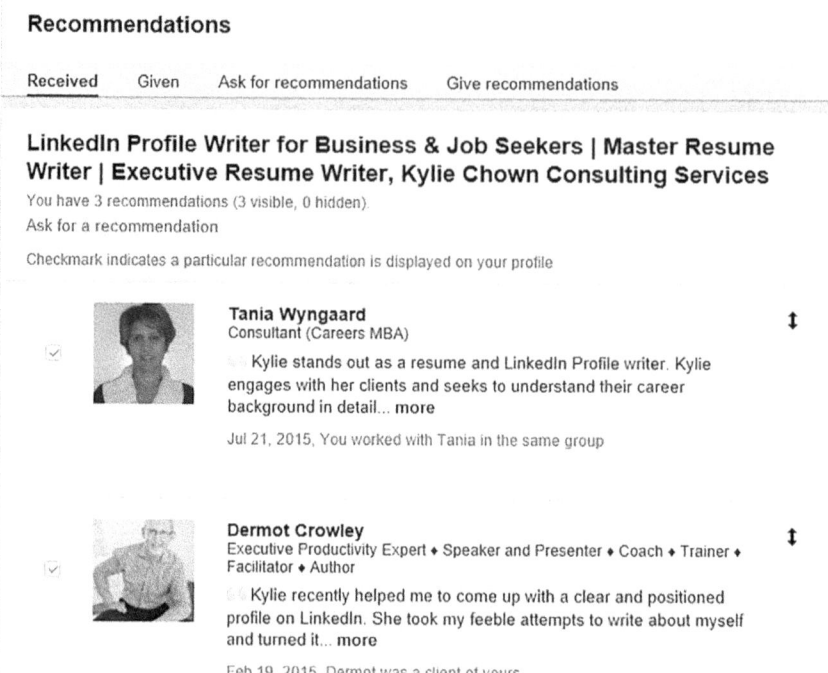

2. Under Given:

You can view all your given recommendations. If you have given a recommendation, you can manage its visibility.

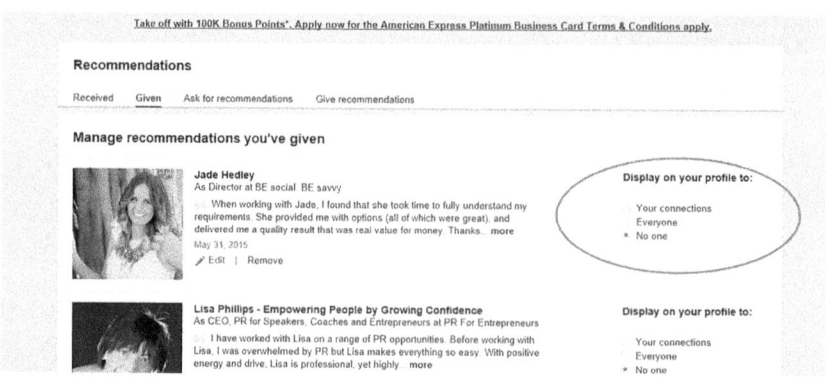

3. **Under Ask for Recommendation:**
Ask your network for recommendations.

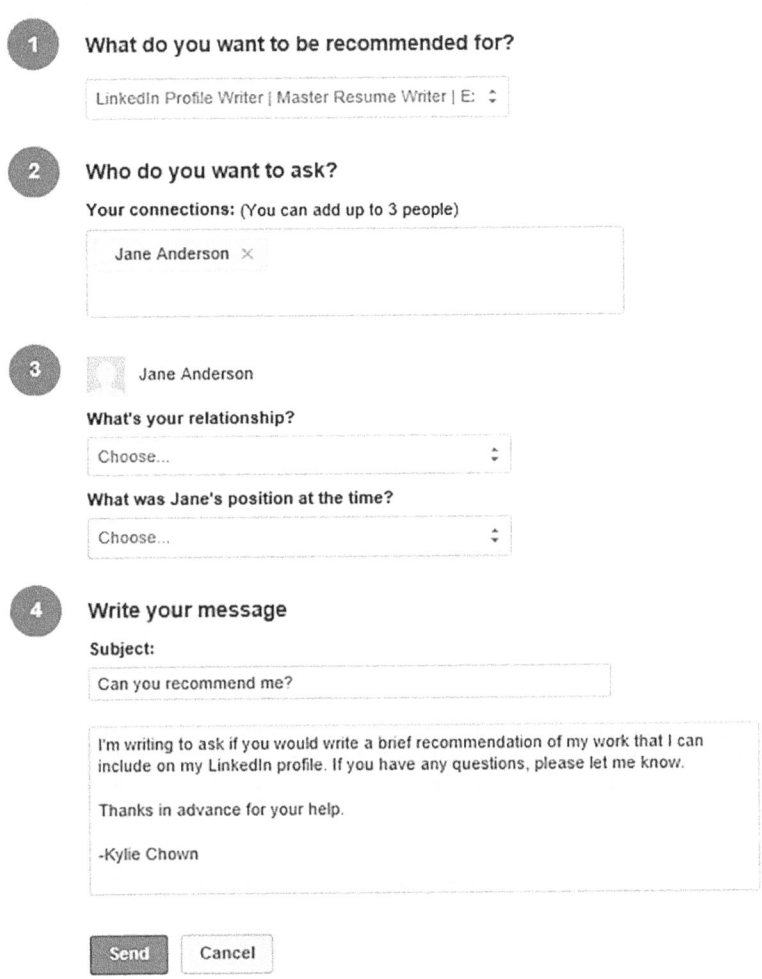

1. Start typing the name of the role you want to be recommended for.
2. Start typing the name of the person you would like to ask.
3. Select your relationship and their position.
4. Write a message and click send.
5. Give Recommendations.

To Give a Recommendation

1. Start typing the name of the person you want to recommend.
2. Select your relationship and positions.
3. Write the recommendation. This is what will appear on their profile. You can also include a message to send.

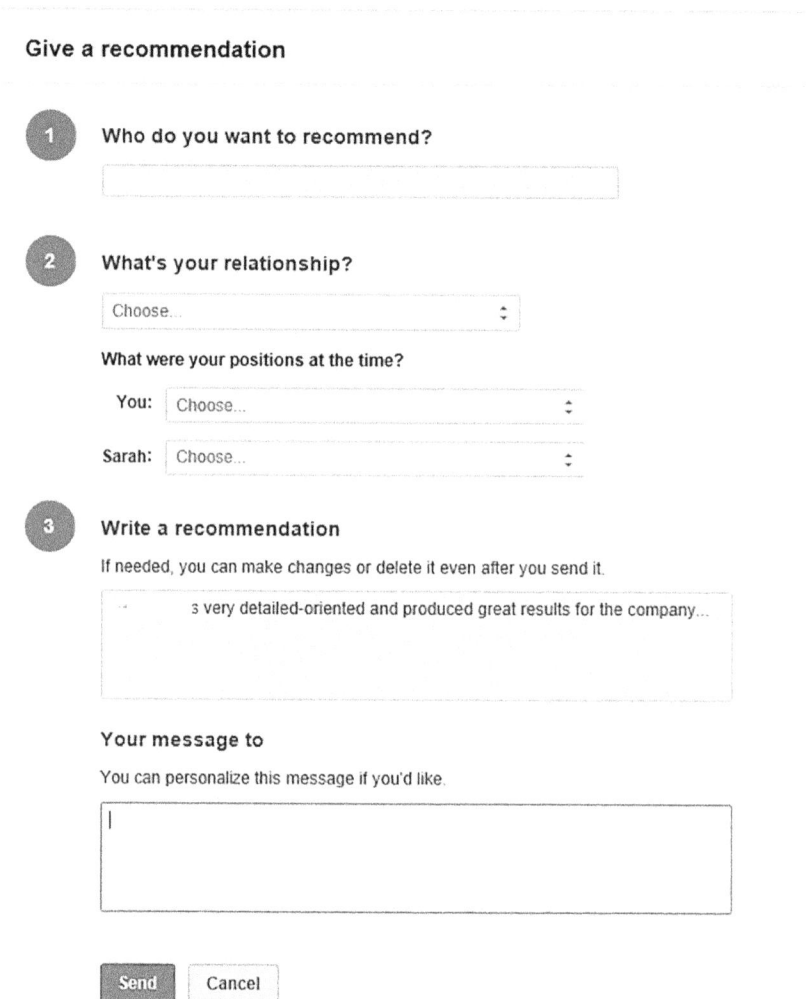

Top Tip #1: Think of the value of a prospective client who sees someone they know and trust recommending your service on LinkedIn.

Top Tip #2: If you do recommend someone, you can hide this on your profile.

Contact Information

I am sure you have had the experience of finding exactly what you were looking for – the perfect product or service – and then couldn't find the necessary contact information or instructions on how to place your order. Quickly, happiness is replaced with frustration. LinkedIn offers a number of ways to manage contact information. You can also include information on websites. To make it easy for people to contact you, look at your contact information in the Edit Contact Information option.

You can see your contact information here:

Once you click on Contact Info:

Click on the pencil icon to change the information.

If you don't have three websites, you can update the information so that it points to three different pages within one website.

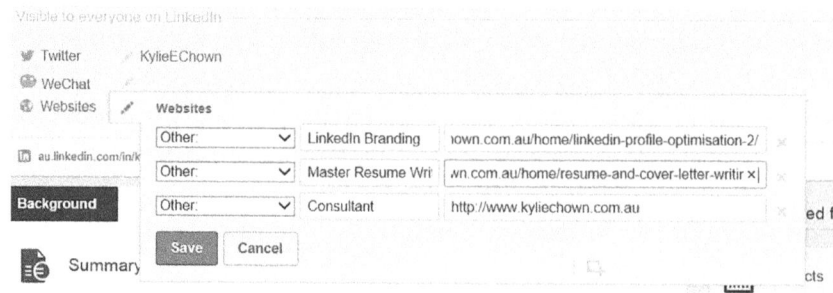

Click [Save]

Industry

The industry you select will also impact your search engine optimisation. Choose the industry you work in, not your job title. For example, if you are an account manager working in the private health sector, you would choose healthcare as opposed to sales and marketing.

Top Tip: Include your contact information as a call to action in your summary. For example: "For more information on how I can help your business, contact me on …"

Settings and Your Profile

How You Are Seen on LinkedIn

After doing all the hard work, it is important that you can be found by your ideal audience. The default position on LinkedIn is to create your profile URL (the web address) with your name and random characters.

The good news is that you can change this. You can create your own vanity URL. This means when someone searches for your name in Google, your LinkedIn profile will be returned. You can also customise how your content is viewed by people who are not connections.

All this can be managed under:

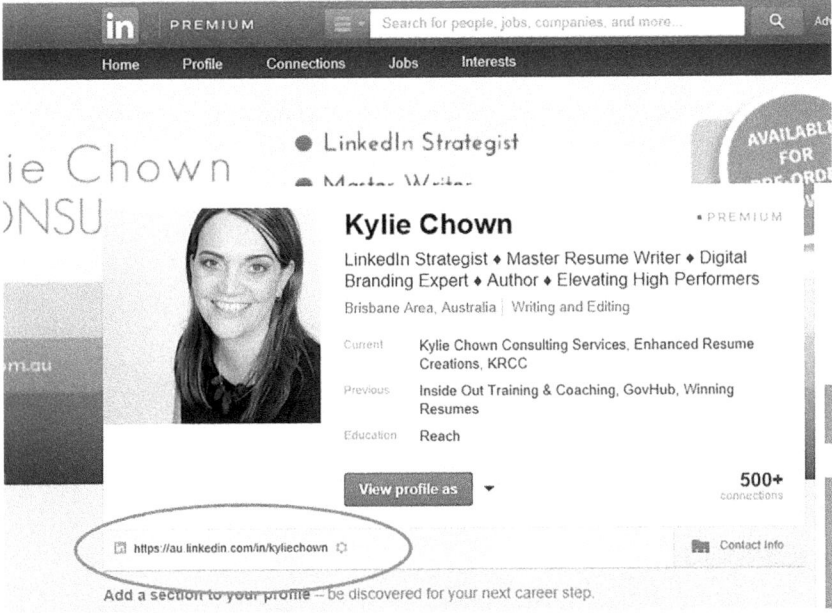

Then on the right you will see:

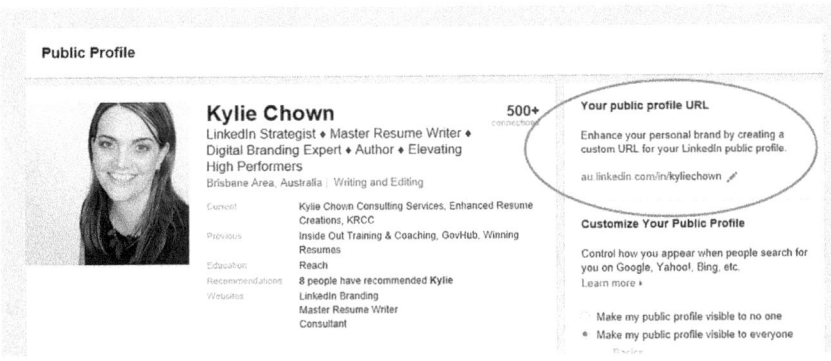

Action Steps

1. Select Edit next to your URL.
2. The next screen provides you with visibility options, as well as an option to change the vanity URL.
3. A ticked box means an area is visible to the public and an unticked box means the area is not publicly visible.
4. You can customise your vanity URL in the circle section above. The vanity URL is what is typed into the web browser. To get to your profile page:

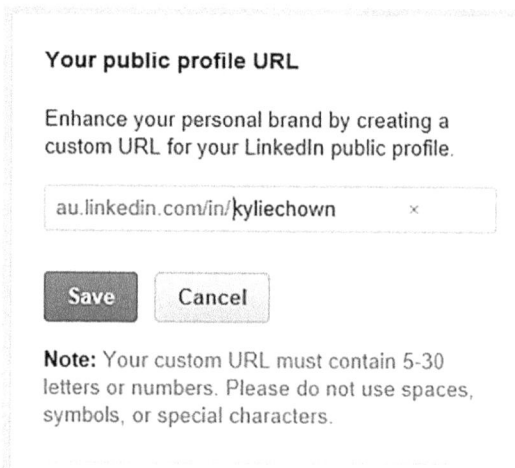

Privacy and Settings

Users have control over how they are presented on LinkedIn.

Under the **Privacy and Settings** option, you will see that you have five main areas you can manage: Profile; Communications; Group, Companies and Applications; and Account.

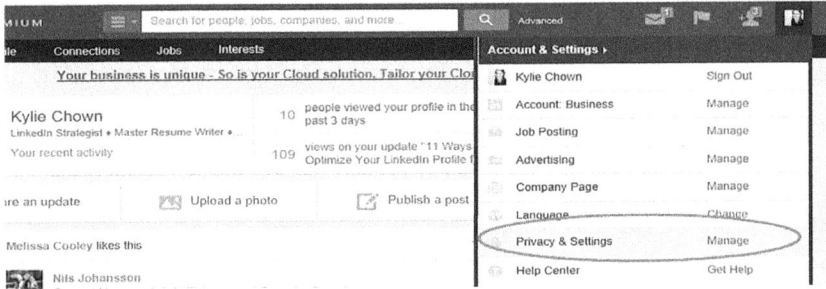

In your **profile tab** you can:

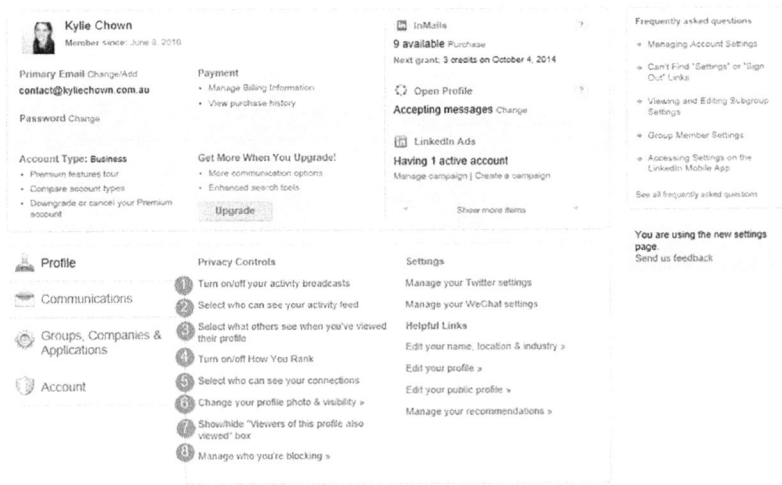

1. **Turn on/off your activity broadcasts.** Use this option if you are making changes to your profile and don't want your network to see them.

2. **Select who can see your activity feed.** You can select Everyone, Your Network, Your Connections or Only You.

3. **Select what others see when you've viewed their profile.** Your Name and Headline, anonymous profile characteristics such as Industry and Title, or you will be totally anonymous.

4. **Turn on/off how you rank.** This is your ranking against competitors.

5. **Select who can see your connections.** In this option, you can decide if your connections can see your other connections. To maintain the privacy of your connections, we recommend you select the Only You option.

6. **Change your profile photo and visibility.** You can change your headshot here.

7. **Show/hide "Viewers of the profile also viewed".** You can see how everyone else is being viewed by your audience.

8. **Manage who you're blocking.** Need to block or report someone? Go to the profile of the person you want to block and select "Block or Report" from the drop-down menu at the top of the profile summary. Note: After you've blocked someone, any previous profile views will disappear from both of your "Who's Viewed My Profile" section.

Additional Tabs Include:

In your communications tab:

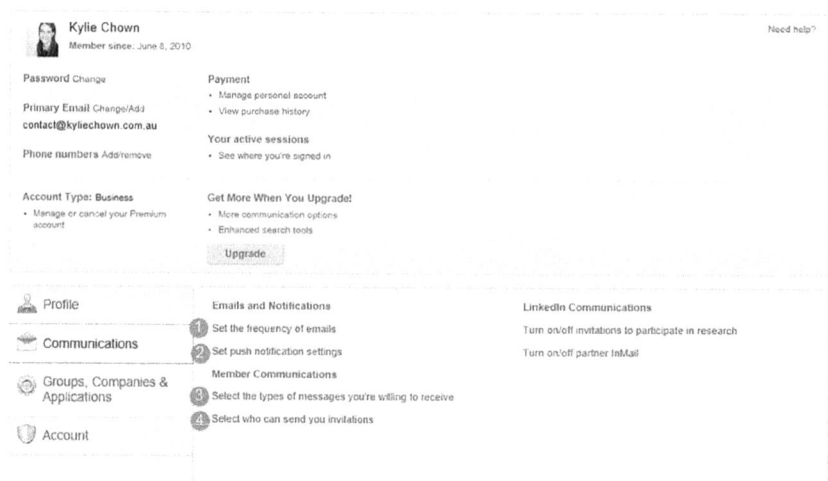

1. Set the frequency of emails.
2. Set push notification.
3. Select the types of messages you're willing to receive.
4. Select those who can send you invitations.

Groups, Companies and Applications allows you to:

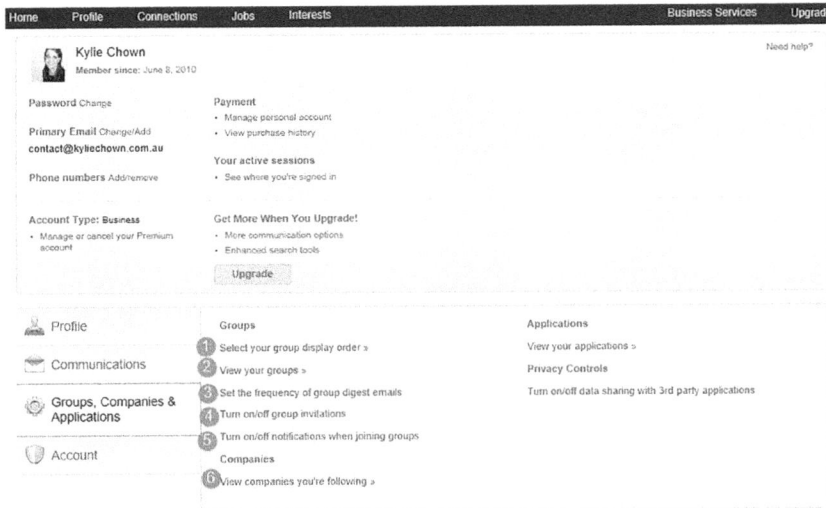

1. Select your group display order.
2. View your groups.
3. Set the frequency of group digest emails.
4. Turn on/off group invitations.
5. Turn on/off notifications when joining groups.
6. View companies you're following.

The Account feature supports privacy controls, while Account allows you to:

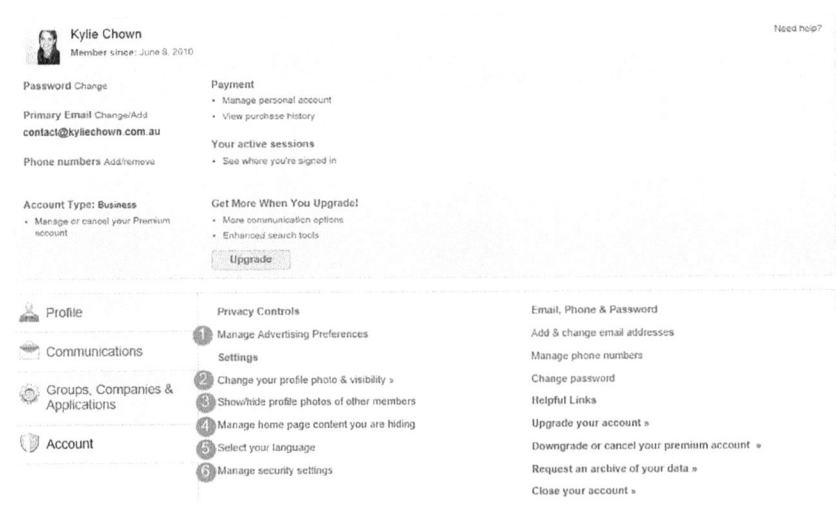

1. Manage Advertising Preferences.
2. Change your profile photo and visibility.
3. Show/hide profile photos of other members.
4. Customise the updates you see on your home page.
5. Select your language.
6. Manage security settings.

Sharing Your Profile

Once you have a customised URL, you can share your profile. Add your LinkedIn URL to your communications (your email signature, newsletters, etc.) so people can easily connect with you. If you are speaking at a conference, seminar or workshop, invite people to connect. At the end of the presentation, you can say something like: "I am on LinkedIn if you would like to connect – just send a request."

Top Tip #1: Did you know that "Who Has Viewed My Profile" is one of the most used features on LinkedIn?

Top Tip #2: Claim your vanity URL quickly – they are all unique and there is only one available for each name.

Reflections and Actions

1. Make a list of all the words you think your ideal client may use when trying to find you.
2. Decide on those that you most enjoy doing and want to be known for.
3. Put those words in your profile and check your search engine optimisation.
4. Perform a Google X-ray search. Note that due to indexing, there may be a time delay in appearing in search results.

Chapter 5

Personal Branding

"My first impressions of people are invariably right."
— *Oscar Wilde*

The first four seconds on your profile are crucial. We only have a short time to connect with the right customer and client you're working with.

It's a bit like touching a hot plate. If your profile doesn't make sense, in other words it's too hot, and the client or person reading your profile will bounce right off.

The Neuroscience of Your Profile

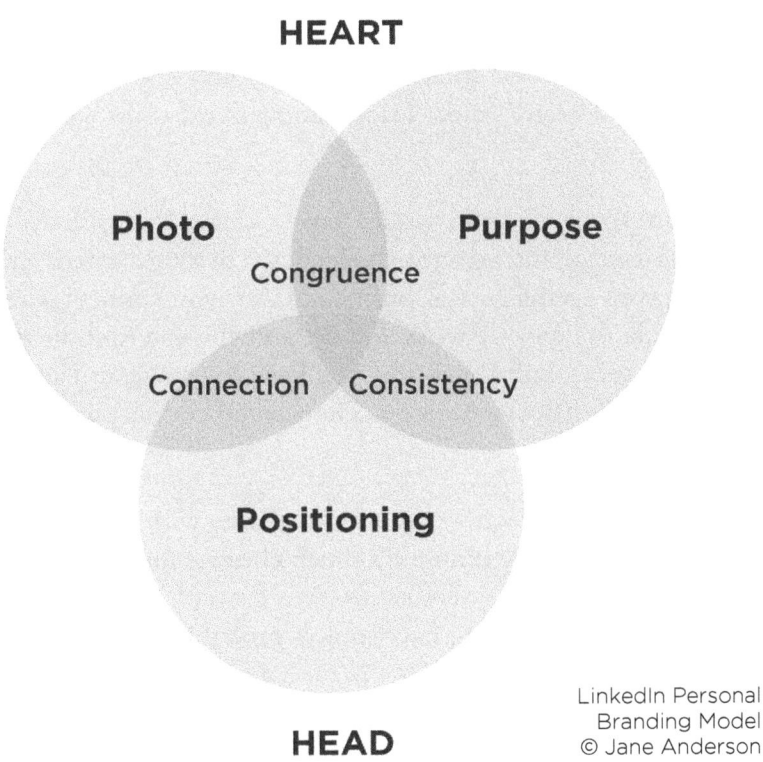

LinkedIn Personal Branding Model
© Jane Anderson

The model above is comprised of three elements:

- **Photo:** Your photo needs to mirror the type of person you want to work with. If it looks unprofessional, then you will attract people who are not necessarily professional. Equally, if it is polished, you will attract that type of client.

- **Positioning:** Positioning is about the customer problems you solve, your credibility and your brand leverage. In other words, it's the level and category that the customer understands you in their mind. It's human nature to categorise people quickly so you need to ensure you are positioned in the right category in the customer's mind.

- **Purpose:** Why do you do what you do? Why does what you do matter? These questions need to be answered early in your profile. Simon Sinek, the author of a number of books including *Start with Why*, says that we need to start with why. This will create rapid cut-through for your reader.

Questions When Someone is Looking at Your LinkedIn Profile

The first questions we are often asked are: "Why should I bother going on LinkedIn? I already have a Facebook page," and, "I don't know that I really want to have any social media presence."

There are a few reasons why you should have a LinkedIn profile. When it comes to running a business, one of the greatest challenges is getting started, and LinkedIn is a great way to help you establish your business. It lets you connect with people who could be interested in the type of work you do, and you can find the demographics of those people. Whereas with Facebook, you have to engage in Facebook marketing (which can be quite expensive) in order to choose and connect with your ideal client's demographics.

LinkedIn is a more cost-effective way of connecting with and researching potential clients if you know what you're doing. It's much cheaper than Facebook, unless you've got a business-to-consumer type of business. For example, if you're a personal trainer working with mums in the suburbs, Facebook is probably the better option, unless you have a lot of corporate clients. If this is the case, a presence on LinkedIn can help. The key question is: "Where does your potential client hang out?"

One of the best things about LinkedIn is that it leverages a Google search. If somebody uses Google to try to find somebody like you, you will turn up in their search results, provided you have excellent search engine optimisation. There are plenty of blogs detailing how to build a search engine optimised LinkedIn profile.

Another reason why you should use LinkedIn is that you can create permanent posts via the blog on your LinkedIn profile. These posts get you in front of your connections so that they don't have to visit your website to read your blog. Don't count on people setting up an RSS feed to your website – it creates too many hurdles for them to keep in touch with you.

Furthermore, LinkedIn lets you keep in touch with your connections without them having to be subscribed to your newsletter. LinkedIn keeps you in touch with the people who are most likely to buy from you. At the moment, there are about 365 million people on LinkedIn.

With the launch of the new students page on LinkedIn, the fastest-growing LinkedIn demographic is university graduates. The most under-represented group on LinkedIn is women.

If you're female, this is a great opportunity as a LinkedIn profile will help you position and market yourself to connect with others.

LinkedIn has grown incredibly to 365 million people having profiles. It was developed in 2003 and is gaining incredible momentum. The problem is, the noise can be a little overwhelming.

The key point to keep in mind is that people buy from people. Many businesses still hold on to the traditional way of doing things. They haven't tapped into social networks, purely because they don't know how to.

Regardless of the role you have, you are Brand You.

You are what makes your brand stand out.

People want to connect with you and like you.

Yes, we have blogs and newsletters, but LinkedIn has arguably been the biggest driver of our businesses' growth and ability to reach out to people.

Some thought leaders, sales people and marketers often fear putting too much self-serving content out there. A lot of people publish content that's about them, and it's not the way to go. LinkedIn has got to be about your audience and what you're doing to help them, not you.

Another challenge you may have is that you have a profile, but you don't know what to write in it. It's completely empty. Perhaps you're unsure of what to write, or think: "What if somebody doesn't like what I have to say?" If this is the case, you need to remember your audience and tell yourself: "I'm here to help people. I have to articulate what it is that I do to help them, and make it easy for them to work with me."

A good place to start is to think about who's reading your content. In Jane's book *IMPACT: How To Build Your Personal Brand for The Connection Economy*, she talks about the First Four Seconds.

When looking at your digital presence, particularly LinkedIn, you only have four seconds for somebody to decide whether they like you or not, and whether they're interested in knowing more.

Something you might be thinking is: "I don't care what's on my profile. I don't care what people think. I'm just going to put anything up there." Brene Brown – TED speaker, expert in vulnerability and author of seven books, including *Daring Greatly* – said: "When you stop caring what people think, you lose your capacity for connection." Connection creates results.

Your job, particularly under "Brand You", is to demonstrate: "I understand your challenges. I have a good knowledge of them. I'm here to help. This is what I can do to help you out of that frustration or pain."

To do this, you must care about what people are reading on your profile, because LinkedIn is all about connection. We're in this age of digital firsts. We often come across someone online before we meet them face to face.

You could be missing an opportunity when you're trying to influence and persuade, when you meet someone face to face, if your LinkedIn profile is not right.

As mentioned earlier, 60 per cent of a buying decision is made before somebody makes contact with you. We want to make it easy for them to think: "Oh yeah, I like this person. I like you. You seem to know what you're doing."

Your profile, in that digital first space we're in now, will either attract or repel a person long before they've even had a chance to meet you.

If your profile is written well, it should answer these questions:

1. **"Why should I care?"** This question creates extraordinary cut-through. Without it, readers will feel as though you're taking them along the yellow brick road and don't know where you're leading them. As Simon Sinek, author of *Start with Why*, says: "People don't buy what you do, they buy why you do it."

Your response to this question needs to be in the first line of your Summary. It hits the reader between the eyes, making them pay attention and wanting to know more!

2. **"Can I see me in you?"** Your profile is a bit like a mirror. When people look at your profile, they're looking to see themselves. "Do you look like the type of person I hang with, or who I would connect with? Do you look a bit like me?" The other thing, too, is your content. Have you written about their problems? Have you written about what your client is looking for? As a potential customer looks at your profile, they ask: "Where is my problem in your profile?" What they want to know is: "Can I see me in you?"

3. **"What makes you different?"** This is about differentiation, and it supports positioning. What do you do differently? Do you work with a particular calibre of clients? Do you work with clients in certain industries? Or the differentiation could be in your message. What is it that differentiates you? Maybe you coach CEOs who have companies of $250 million-plus. What makes you different?

4. **"How will what you do benefit me?"** For example, you might say: "I'm an expert in environmental engineering. How I help people, how I support you, is that I reduce your organisation's emissions by 25 per cent, so that you can be an environmentally responsible organisation." You need to articulate how people can benefit from what you have to offer.

5. **"Do you understand my world?"** This is about their problems. This is about clearly articulating the problems your potential client or customer has. If you don't show that you understand their world and your profile is all about you, then people will feel you're not going to listen to them.

6. **"Who have you worked with that I know?"** This is where brand leverage comes into play, because not everybody knows you. But they will get a better understanding of you if you have worked with an organisation they are familiar with, particularly if the organisation has a big name or brand. You might say something like: "Some of the clients I have worked with include ..." The reader might not know you, but they know and trust those well-established companies. It's brand association: "Who have you worked with that I know? That will give me trust."

7. **"What do people say about you?"** You might notice the recommendations at the bottom of your LinkedIn profile. This area is where the reader gets to see you through somebody else's eyes – not through your eyes. It helps people get to know you better. According to the 2012 Carer Builder Survey, if a recruiter or

hiring manager likes your personality, 50 per cent of the time they'll extend an offer. Now while we might be saying here, "We're not recruiting," the same thing happens for salespeople and solopreneurs, because they face the same challenges in their marketing. If you can get your personality to come through on as many angles as possible, you're more likely to connect.

8. **"How effective have you been? What results have you been able to achieve?"** You'll need to give reference to a particular program you deliver to clients and what they have said. You need to show the results you have achieved and how. Testimonials can help capture your achievements.

9. **"Who has said that you're any good?"** This can, in part, be answered by your recommendations, but you also may also have testimonials on your website that you can plug in to your profile. Let's say I'm a coach and I need a graphic designer. You're a graphic designer and I'm on your LinkedIn profile. If I see a testimonial from Mary Smith, executive coach, Sydney, I'm going to think: "Oh, well, this person understands what a coach is after." If you want to work with a certain industry, make sure your testimonials are from people in that industry.

10. **"What's your perspective?"** Your perspective will help the person understand or connect with your personality. Your perspective is evident in your blog posts. The great thing about LinkedIn is that your posts are permanent. They don't just pass through your feed like a normal update. Potential clients can read your previous posts, get your perspective, and decide whether or not to work with you. For example, if you are an HR consultant who has written about performance management and leadership, someone going through your posts and articles may think: "Oh yeah, he thinks like us. I think we could work together. I like that he said that, because that's exactly the challenge we're having."

11. **"How do I work with you?"** One of the basic things often missing from a LinkedIn profile is the answer to the question: "How do I work with you?" All you have to do is say: "If you'd like to work with me, here's my phone number," or, "Here's my website." Make it easy for people to understand how they can work with you. Don't be over the top or too creative. Just make it practical and straightforward, and let them connect.

12. **"Where can I find more information?"** Make sure you include your phone number, website and email address. Bear in mind that when you're on your LinkedIn profile and on your page, in the contact us area you'll see where the contact information drops down. It sits under your photo and under the title. A lot of people don't realise that's where to go to find your contact information.

Make sure you have it loud and clear in your summary area. It will use up a few characters, but it's worth it.

13. **"Are you a fake account?"** What makes your profile look fake and prevents people from connecting with you is not having an employment history and not having any recommendations, skills and endorsements. It looks particularly suspicious if you have, say, 500 connections and none of them have endorsed you. Make sure your profile has as much information as possible to help people trust and connect with you. By the way, LinkedIn is fantastic at responding quickly if someone has taken your profile photo or if you have any concerns.

If you can address these questions in your profile, you'll get your first four seconds working for you. People will find you interesting and be excited about connecting with you.

Your Photo

"A picture is worth a thousand words."
– Napoleon Bonaparte

When Jane started her first business, she asked a friend to take her photo for her website. It was a nice photo with a tree in the background. There was natural light and it was a nice, sunny day.

Jane used the photo in her branding and noticed she got clients who didn't really see that she was serious. It was as though she was working on a hobby. Jane progressed to a professional headshot, which helped, but the photo still looked a little washed out and too soft. She felt as though the clients seeing her were looking for someone soft and understanding, and she can be. But her ideal client was someone who wanted more, was motivated to get it and wanted practical steps to make it happen; not someone who just wanted a counsellor to have a chat to.

Your headshot will create an emotional connection with the person looking at it and you need to be mindful of the context in which your photo is seen:

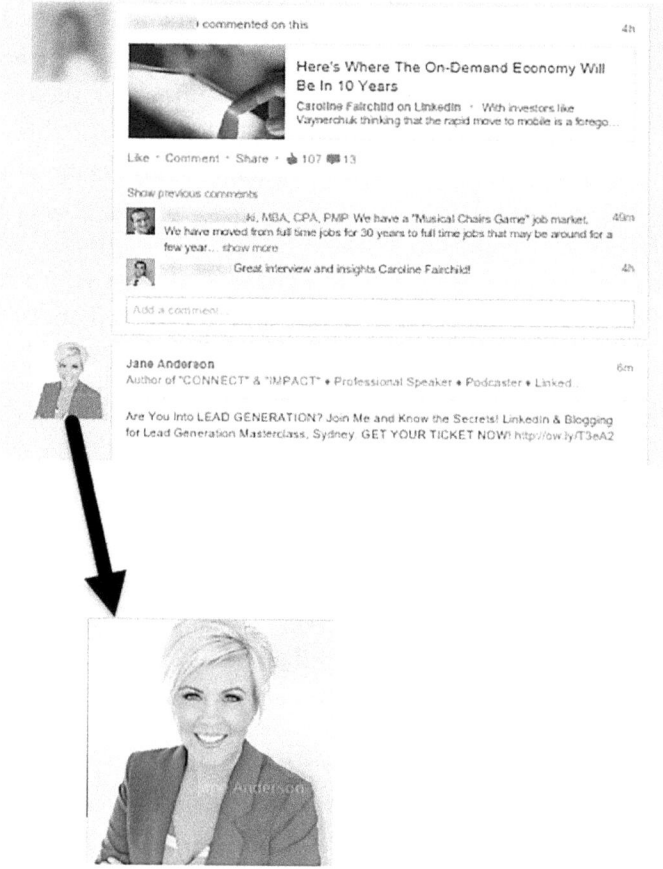

In this case, there are some issues:

- The colour means the image stands out. Black and white would play down the image and blend in too much, especially on LinkedIn.
- The photos that stand out the most are brightly coloured.
- The person in this photo is close and easy to recognise. If the image was too far away, it would be difficult to recognise in a LinkedIn feed.

Jane recently worked with a client who insisted on keeping a photo of himself speaking on stage as his LinkedIn profile picture. He was so far away in the picture that she could hardly see him, but he wanted to be known for speaking and thought this photo was relevant. His thinking was right, but the photo was better suited for a website than a LinkedIn profile picture as it was so small.

Something we don't always remember is that LinkedIn has many other distractions when someone looks at your profile. Ads, recommended connections or connections in common hamper the decision maker's analytical ability, so your profile needs to stand out from the noise on screen.

A recent study by The Ladders shows that decision makers tend to follow a consistent path when reviewing online profiles, so the organisation of your layout is crucial. As much as 19% of the time someone spends looking at your profile will be spent looking at your photo! To get a high return on investment on that time, consider the following:

1. **Does your photo portray what you're trying to achieve?** If you are wearing a suit in your picture, you will attract ambitious corporate clients. If you have soft, flowing fabrics, you will attract softer people. It sounds obvious, but you will get back what your photo portrays, more so than your text.

2. **Remember the context of your photo.** It needs to stand out in a feed. Too many people think their photo is seen in the context of their profile, rather than in someone's feed. Remember, your photo may be in the context of a comment or discussion. Many people will view your photo on a page other than your profile page.

3. **It is not a glamour shot.** It is not where you get your long, soft, flowing locks out, and you shouldn't use a photo of yourself in an evening gown or wedding suit. It is a corporate, professional business photo.

4. **Look at the camera.** Wistfully looking away does nothing to personalise your potential connection. Create chemistry with the reader by looking at the lens.

5. **Props should only be used if they convey your goal.** For example, if you're a photographer, you can have a camera. If you're a saxophonist, you can have a saxophone in the shot. If you're a speaker only, yes, you can have a microphone in your hand if your goal is to speak. If you want to be well-rounded, just have a picture of yourself. You will receive what you ask for, so be clear about the message your photo sends.

6. **Have a headshot on all your social media.** No blank heads or eggs! We know that a profile with a headshot will have seven times more click-through than a profile without a headshot.

7. **Make sure it's a clear headshot from your chest to the top of your head.** In other words, no full-body shots or anything where people can't recognise you if they met you at an event or on the run.

8. **Smile and show teeth.** It makes you look open and friendly, helping your "know, like and trust" perception amplify.

9. **Make sure you don't have sunglasses on.** You can look as though you have something to hide or are a bit "shady" – pardon the pun!

10. **You get what you pay for.** If you're trying to get a million-dollar client, you need to look like a million-dollar expert. Invest in a professional shot that mirrors what you're asking of your client.

By investing in a great headshot, you'll stand out and people will feel as though they already know you, making the sales or recruitment processes easier. If you have a tight budget, prepare to spend about $300 for a good professional shot. If you are ready to step it up in your business, invest in a higher-quality photographer and make-up artist. You can expect to pay $600-$2000 for a series of highly targeted shots to use in articles, brochures, newsletters, webpages and other marketing collateral. These shots need to mirror your business goals for the next three years.

By putting in a little bit of effort, your professional photos will pay dividends and generally last you three years.

Action Steps to Add a Photo

Log in to your account. Click Profile.
1. Click Edit Profile.

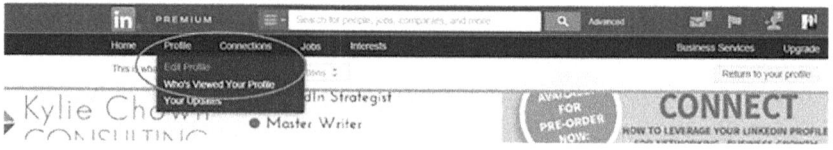

2. Click Change Photo and hover the cursor over your headshot. You will see an image of a camera and Change Photo.

3. Click Change Photo.

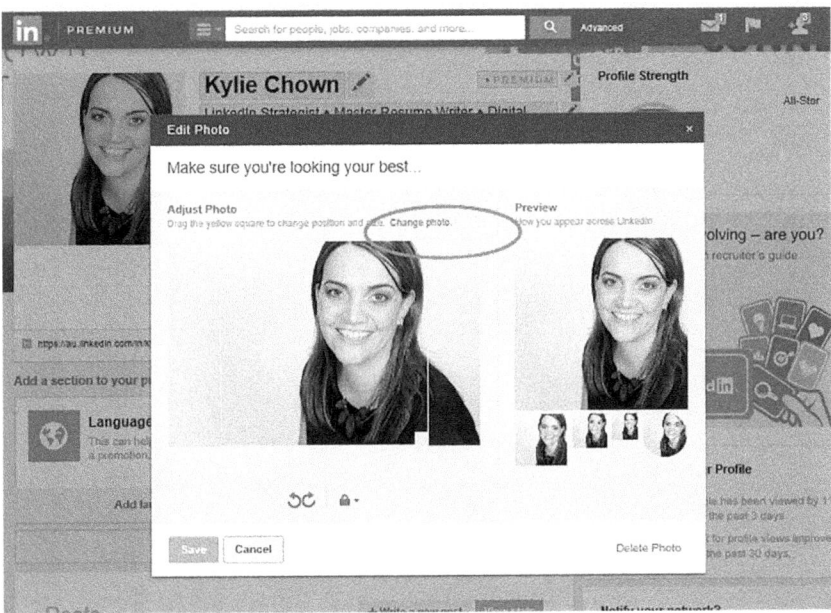

4. Select the photo you want, then open.

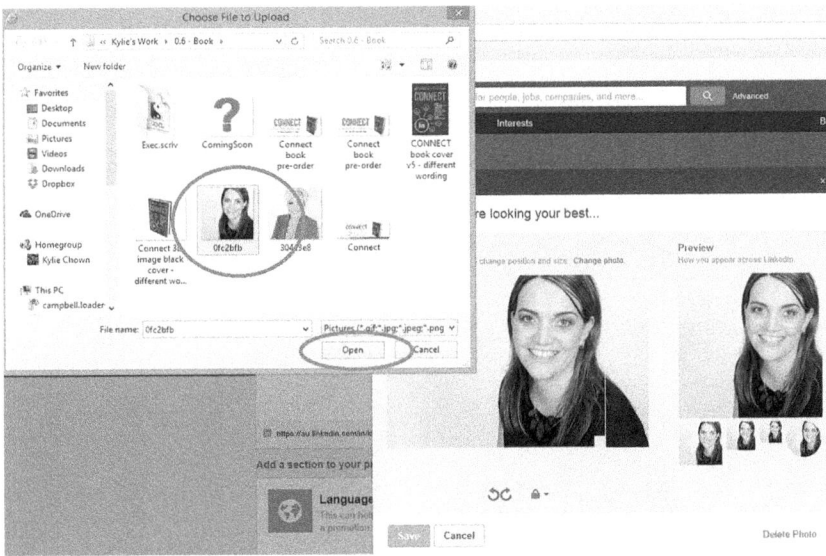

5. Click Save

Other Sections

LinkedIn offers you a range of additional sections to further enhance your profile. You can target the sections that best suit your requirements. These include:

Education

In your Education section, you can add anything that supports your ongoing development.

   Under Education, click on Add Education.

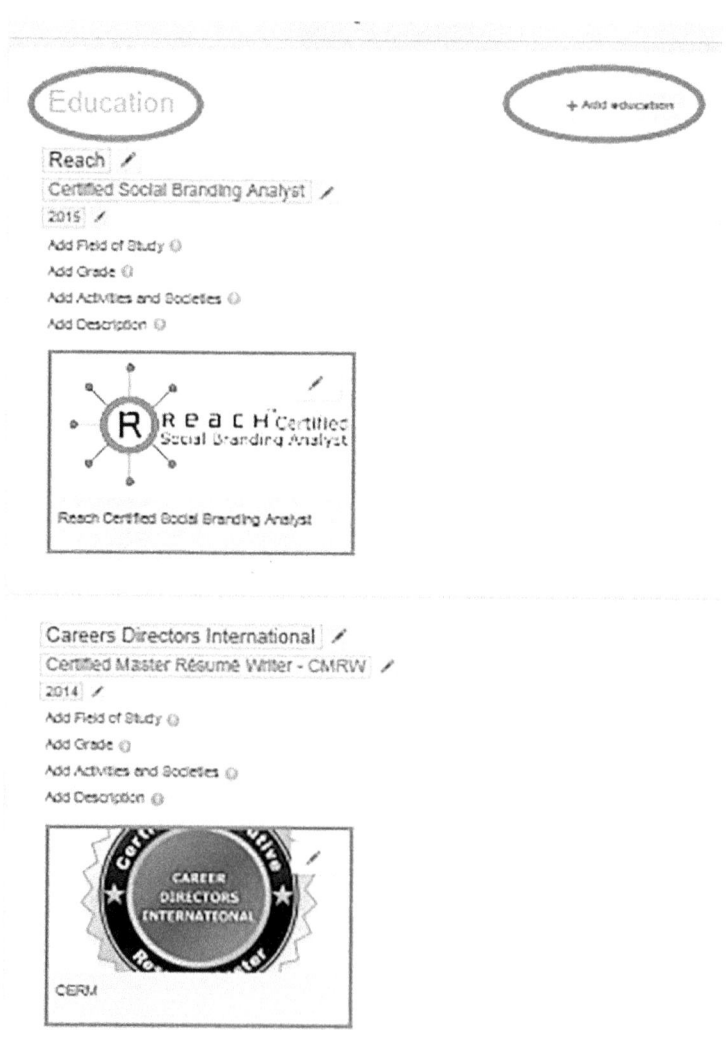

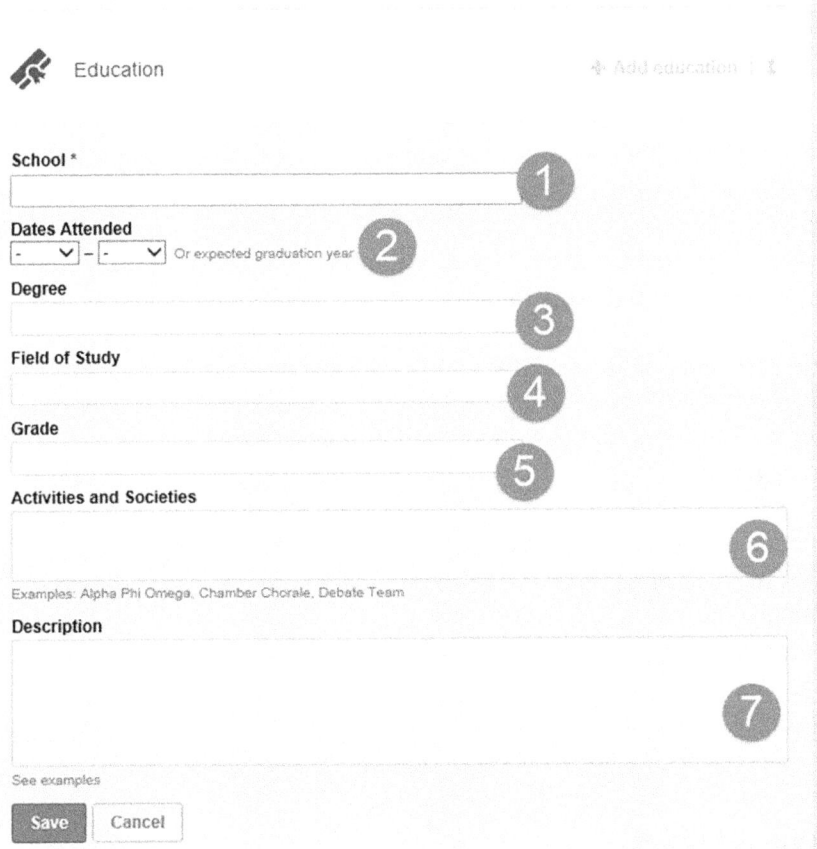

Action Steps

To complete the Education section:

1. Add the school you attended. You will see there is a drop-down menu within this area.
2. Enter the dates you attended.
3. Enter the degree you studied.
4. Enter the field of study.
5. Enter the grade (this is not a compulsory field).
6. Explain any activities and societies you were involved in.
7. Add a description of your course.

Other Sections You Can Add to Your LinkedIn Profile Include:

- **Organisations:** This area can be utilised to highlight participation in industry groups or professional associations. This supports you as an expert in your field.

- **Volunteering and Causes:** If you volunteer in an area that resonates with your ideal audience, include this here.

- **Certifications:** Include certifications relevant to your area of expertise.

- **Projects:** This area allows you to highlight collaborations and projects you have been a part of.

You also have the option to include:

- Languages
- Honours and awards
- Test scores
- Patents

Commenting

When commenting on something in your feed, always be positive and ask yourself: "Is my comment constructive and helpful, or is it supportive?" You can certainly challenge things, but be mindful of your language and tone. Don't swear or use put downs, otherwise you risk being removed from LinkedIn.

You can also tag people's names in your comments to include them or draw attention.

Recently, we had a client who was a coach in Sydney. She commented on an article about coaching in the workplace, saying: "Well, based on my experience, I think the challenge is this …" and wrote something insightful. Somebody else contacted her as a result of that comment and said, "Look, I really like what you said in your comment. We haven't met. I'd love to have a coffee with you." And they've ended up doing a lot of work together.

Commenting on an article or post allows you to share your experience and demonstrate to others your knowledge without having to say: "I'm so good." It's easier, too, isn't it?

How to Comment

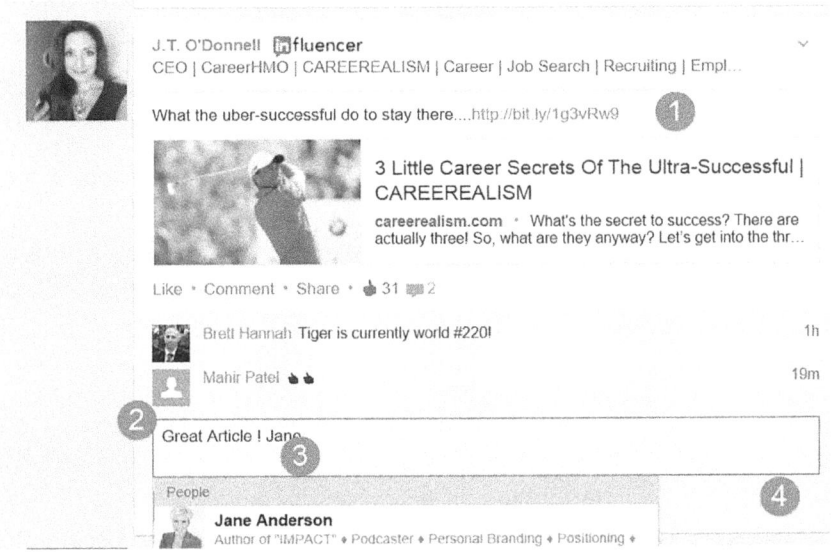

1. Identify something to comment on when you scroll through your newsfeed.
2. Write your comment.
3. To tag someone, start typing their name and click on them from the list.
4. You can then click the comment box.

Curatorship

Jane once said: "When I was little, I remember trying to talk my Dad into things I wanted, like new shoes or a new cassette (yes, I'm showing my age!), but it didn't always go too well because Mum was the boss and was in charge of those types of decisions! So I soon worked out that if I said that Mum said I could have it, Dad would listen because he trusted my Mum, of course. Otherwise, it was just me banging on again about something I wanted. The power of being able to influence an outcome was not so much about me asking for it, but the value of the *right* person saying it."

Content curation in social media provides the same influence. A content curator is a bit like a museum curator. A museum curator decides what artefacts go into the museum for people to see. Their job is to research and know what people are looking for so they visit. The curator's knowledge, expertise and experience are most valuable to a museum's success. So as a content curator, your skills are highlighted by the content you share in your social media.

After delivering some workshops recently, we discovered that many clients are reluctant to share their content because they feel it should be on their own blog, and they end up with less visibility. They don't believe curation has as much value, when in fact curation can be even more valuable. President of the Queensland Chapter of the Australian Marketing Association, Kellie-Ann Robinson, recently shared her insight that a new role will start to emerge in organisations called a "Content Curator", and this will be a public relations role.

There are four big reasons why content curation works:

1. **Someone else has said it:** The fact that it wasn't just said by you means your opinion is validated by other experts in your field. You're therefore opening yourself to being more trusted.

2. **You get to contrast your insights:** You can combine multiple pieces of information to curate and share your insights. You can still add your expertise, even if you don't agree with what is being said.

3. **Less "salesy":** Instead of constantly pumping out your own content and being too self-promoting, you can leverage what others say and genuinely add value to your audience. Let's face it, we don't like having sales talk shoved down our throat in feeds all day.

4. **It's more efficient:** You spend less time writing content from scratch and more on your insights. This means you can share more, add more value and increase your visibility.

You might be thinking: "Well, if I share other people's insights, won't I just be sending clients to them?" Not necessarily. It depends if they're a direct competitor and what they do. Some experts only write, so if you're a coach, you won't be competing. Equally, if you're in business development, you're looking for independent sources to validate your insights.

If you can allocate a few minutes to curate content each day, it will boost your visibility. You can even get your virtual assistants and marketing teams to help manage it. It's also an easy way to be consistent, making it easier for the reader to understand what you do and how you can help them. Not doing it means your competition will work with your customers before you do.

Scoop.it is a great curation site. It will email you content and articles to curate. You can sign in and put in the keywords you are interested in. It will then email your links to articles. The website address is http://www.scoop.it/

How to Curate

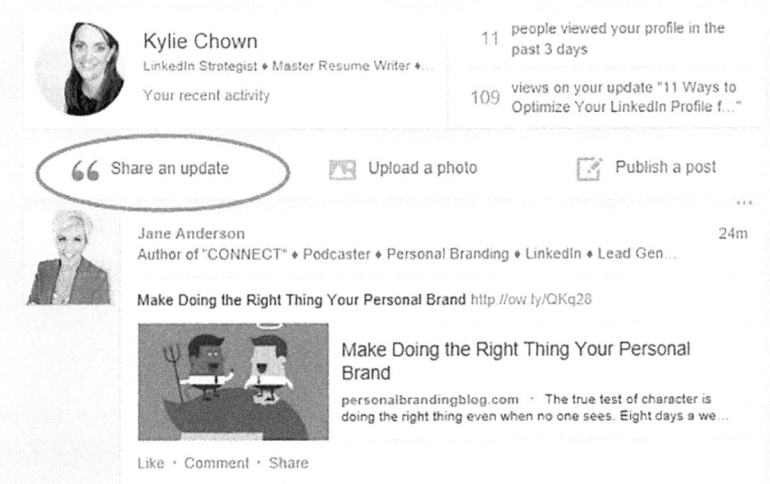

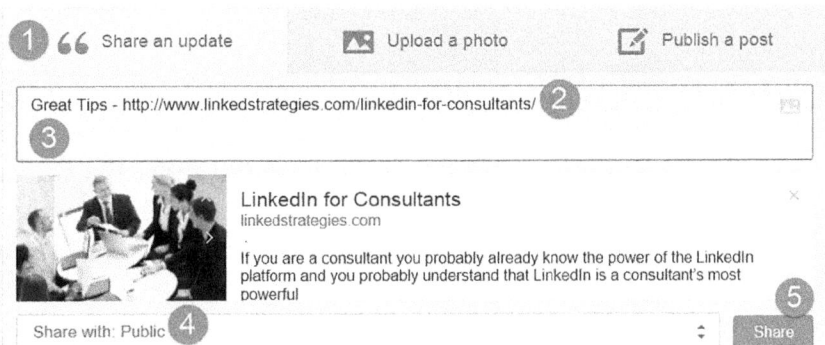

1. Click Share an Update.
2. Copy the URL you want to share.
3. You can make a comment before the article you are sharing.
4. Determine who you want to share it with: Public, Public + Twitter, or Just Your Connections.
5. Click Share.

Thought Leadership

You may have been wondering why there are so many different people posting on LinkedIn now, not just Richard Branson and James Caan. LinkedIn now allows anyone to post their content to become an influencer. The question we're being asked is: "What do I write? Is there a framework or formula?"

We need to write what we know so that we can amplify our message and give to others more efficiently. If you have enough of a profile online, you should get multiple views in a few hours after posting an article. Posting regularly on LinkedIn works hand-in-hand with other profile-building tools such as Twitter.

There are two ways your thought leadership validates and works for you on LinkedIn:

Notifications: This serves to share your insights and ideas. It also allows you to stay visible to your audience. Your connections will continue to see your posts as they receive a notification to say that you have written a new post.

Validation: When a potential client lands on your profile, they may read your posts based on your thought leadership. This helps them gain an understanding of you and your approach. It allows them to connect and determine if you understand their issues and challenges, and to identify how in-tune you really are.

Content Strategy

Jane has a friend who is a photographer. She takes beautiful shots, but she pushes her book in her newsfeed about three times per day. It feels as though the audience is just there to serve the purpose of buying her book. On the other hand, if she gave some tips on why good photography is important and how pictures need to tell different stories, then not only does the audience get a glimpse of what might be in the book, they might buy it and recommend it to others.

Your content strategy is not about you. It's about your customers and being visible to them. A good way to start doing this is to write a list of your areas of expertise that you can share with people.

Ensure you link your content strategy to what you're trying to achieve. If in the next 12 months you want to position yourself as a thought leader on innovation, what are your key areas of expertise related to innovation?

Have a call to action/service for every time you post content. It's recommended you "sell" once per week, or 20% of your time.

Jane recently shared: "Last month, I found myself looking for a new car. It was late on a Friday and I was rushing around, trying to find the best deal. I'd done all my online research and ended up at a particular dealer. He sensed I needed to decide on the car quickly, as it was the end of the financial year, so he let me take it home for the weekend to try it out. This certainly eased some pressure for me. I didn't have to rush my decision; I could drive the car for the weekend and return it on Monday. The dealer wasn't pushy. He was helpful, listened to my needs and made the whole process easy. As a result, I decided to keep the car."

According to *Forbes*, 60% of a buying decision is made before the customer buys from you. Similarly, the CareerBuilder Survey found that 58% of recruiters extended a job offer because they got a good sense of the job seeker's character and personality.

If you're a consultant, coach, job seeker, mentor, salesperson or solopreneur, one of the best ways to encourage people to test drive YOU is to write a blog. It's a bit like being allowed to take the car overnight. Your posts take the reader from their world into yours. They give the reader your insights and perspective. Too often, we want the customer or recruiter to make a decision there and then, and we risk looking pushy or salesy, or making the customer feel weird about the whole situation.

Seth Godin, author of 17 books including *Tribes*, says we're in the connection economy. People want to connect and buy you, but they will buy when they're ready.

We've all come across the stereotypical car dealer who just wants to get their commission. But we need to get to know the car first. "Will it give me what I need? Will be it economical enough? Do I like it? Is it safe?" Your client or recruiter is asking these same questions. Organisations don't have extra cash floating around if things go wrong, so every dollar matters.

As F.W. Woolworth, the founder of Woolworth Corporation, said: "I am the world's worst salesperson so I must make it easy for people to buy."

Allow people to get to know you. Give samples of your work through your blog so there is less pressure on you to sell.

Being a LinkedIn Poster

One of the more recent changes to LinkedIn has been the capability for anyone to write posts. Previously, the role of a poster was reserved for approximately 500 professionals, including the likes of Richard Branson, Bill Gates, Arianna Huffington and Guy Kawasaki. Now, anyone can be a poster on LinkedIn.

Why be a poster on LinkedIn?

- **Increased exposure across the platform:** If you publish a post on LinkedIn, it can be shared, liked and commented on. This in turn increases your exposure across LinkedIn.

- **Engage your target audience:** LinkedIn gives you the opportunity to talk directly to your target audience through posting.

- **Thought leadership:** Establish yourself as an expert in your field by posting articles.

- **Support SEO:** SEO optimised blog posts contribute to your SEO and are shown within search results.

Here are a few things to remember when writing articles if you have a premium LinkedIn account:

- **It's not Facebook.** Posting on LinkedIn is different to posting pictures on your Facebook page. LinkedIn is not the forum to post pictures, inspiring quotes or memes. This is a space for you to share your professional expertise and provide good-quality content.

- **Don't attach your newsletter as a Word document to your feed and think anyone will read it.** This is not posting information in a way that engages your audience. Put the newsletter content in the post area so it is there permanently and paints a clear picture of who you are for anyone who clicks on your profile. It also helps to build the "know, like and trust" factor you're trying to achieve.

- **A post can be as long as you like.** To engage your reader, keep it to the point. Ideally, stick to 400-600 words.

To begin with, there are a few elements your LinkedIn posts need to provide to your readers:

- Why what you have to say is important.
- Evidence to back your claims.
- A formula your readers can use for success.
- A call to action.

So if you're not a writer, how can you write effective posts? Gihan Perera, author of Fast, Flat and Free and 10 other books on internet marketing, suggests a method that we recommend to most novices. This method is called the PILES method.

The PILES method covers:

- **Principle/Problem/Purpose:** What is the point of the article? You need to give it context, so it could be a story, an analogy or recent research.

- **Implications:** What happens if you don't do it? Add hyperlinks to provide evidence to back your claims. It might be some research or an article from a credible source in your industry. Alternatively, you could detail implications the topic has for a particular industry.

- **List:** List steps to overcome the problem. Keep the list simple and easy to read. Lists with a prime number of steps allow you to easily market your steps in the heading of your post. Prime numbers jump off the screen and catch a reader's attention more easily.

- **Explanation:** Explain each step in a sentence or two. Explain what the benefit or impact each item in the list will have.

- **Summary:** Write a conclusion. This gives emphasis to the point you're trying to make. We also recommend writing a call to action here. For example, provide a link to a landing page on your website. It can be frustrating for your readers if they get to the end of an article and decide they need help, but the article fails to provide information on where to find it.

If you can stick to writing posts daily, in less than two months you will have a book on your hands! A book is a great way to position yourself an expert in your field. We also recommend using an image in your header that reflects the point you're trying to make. The image will be added to your profile and makes it more appealing for your reader to click through to your post.

To write a post, log in to your LinkedIn profile and:

1. Click Profile.
2. Edit Profile.

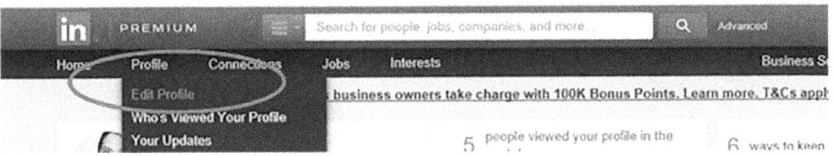

3. You will see "Share an update", "Upload a photo" and "Publish a Post". Click on Publish a Post.

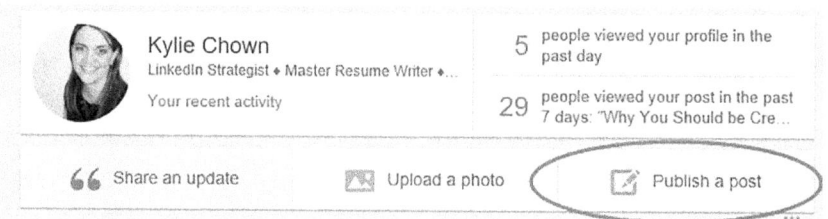

Action Steps to Write a Post

1. Add a title.
2. Write your post.
3. Format your post.
4. Add a hyperlink.
5. Add an image.
6. Save the post (note: this will not publish).
7. Publish the post.

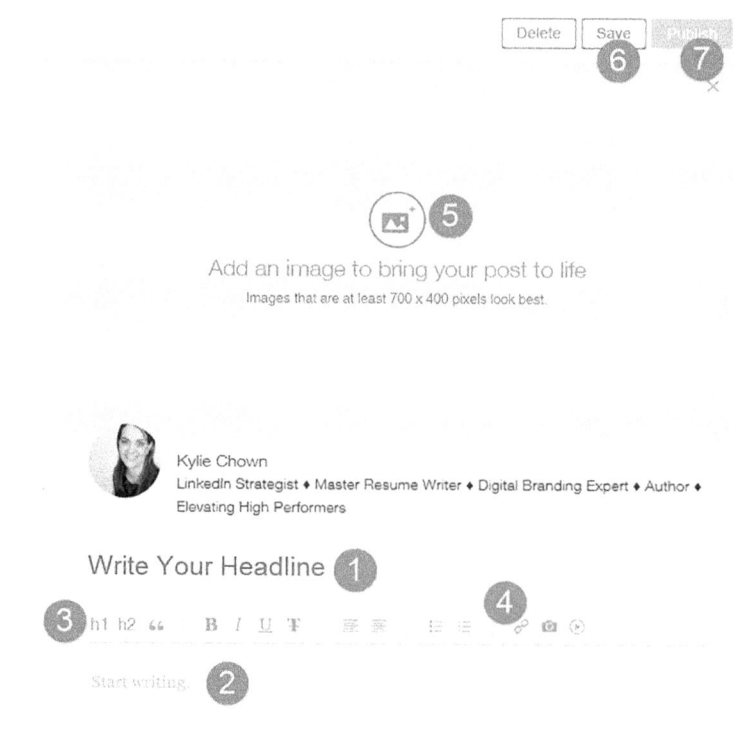

Groups and Companies

LinkedIn gives you the option to join groups and follow companies. This is a great way to find out information about your industry.

Within each group, there are discussions. You can use group discussions to:
- Position yourself as an expert in your field by providing information on your area of expertise and answering questions posted in groups. You can sort discussions to quickly identify discussions around your area of expertise.
- Obtain information by starting a discussion within a group.
- Increase exposure across your network with improved visibility.
- Join groups where your ideal customers and prospects are. You can contribute to discussions as an industry leader and engage with your targeted customers in an organic way.
- Improve your knowledge base by leveraging other leaders in the industry.
- Conduct market research and get a true sense of the current situation.
- Create a link to a potential connection. You can use the common group status if you are requesting to connect with someone.

Some guidelines around contributing to discussions in groups:

- Groups are for knowledge building and sharing. Make sure your posts are genuine and do not advertise your company's products or services.
- Remember your manners. Engage as you would in a face-to-face situation and remember that written material can be interpreted differently, so write in a clear and concise manner.

You will see your groups listed at the bottom of your profile page. Groups are like a branding exercise because they give people looking at your profile an idea of what you're interested in.

Groups also increase your proximity to your connections. You will turn up in the search result of a particular topic if you're part of a related group.

Running a group is a big job. There are benefits, but a lot of work is involved. It may be more worth your while to remain a contributor.

What does a contributor mean? A contributor means you can join a group and contribute to the discussion by posting your articles, posing questions and providing answers. Being a contributor to a group can open networks to you. It's easier to attract the attention of someone who is in a group you are a member of.

We said 40-60 per cent of connections that convert for you ideally come from direct introductions. Ten to 20 per cent ideally come from groups and 5 to 10 per cent are from direct emails, and that's you making direct approaches.

You need to customise your approach. For example, you could say: "Hi there. I thought I'd offer to connect. I noticed that we're in this particular group. I help people like you and would it be helpful if I sent you some information? Would it be helpful if I had a coffee with you?"

Action Steps

Some groups are open, meaning anyone can join, and some closed, meaning you need to be approved to join.

In the search box at the top of any page, select Groups from the drop-down list on the left. Type in your keywords or group name to search.

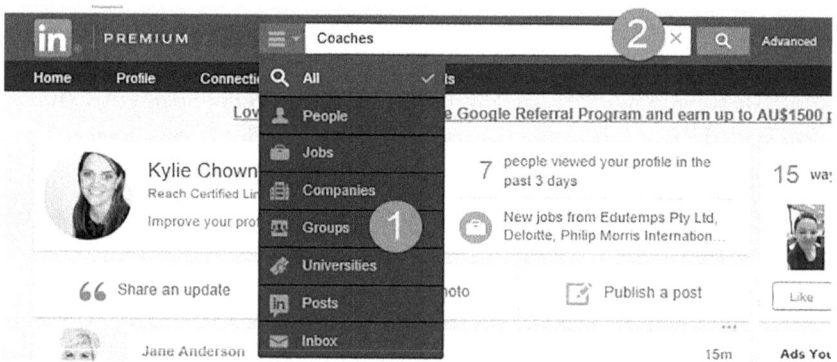

Once you have found a group you would like to join, click on the title and then:

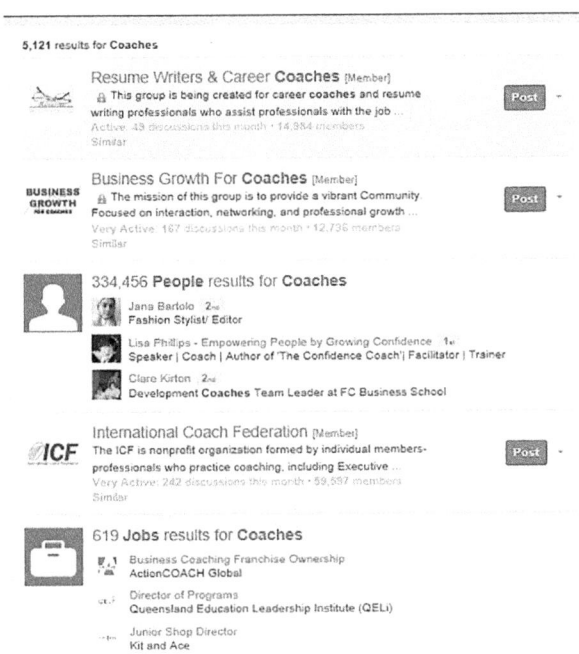

1. This is the title of the group.
2. This is a description of the group. This will often tell you what the group is about, who it is suitable for and any guidelines you should consider before you join.
3. This lists members of the group who are currently within your network.
4. "About this group" provides you with the group's statistics.
5. Once you have reviewed the information, click the join button if you would like to join.

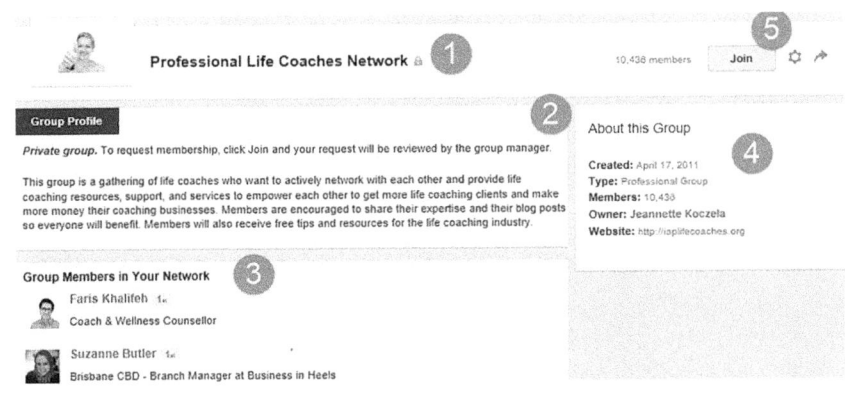

Once you have set your groups, it is a good idea to manage the communication for the group. You can do this by:

Logging in to your account.
Clicking Profile.

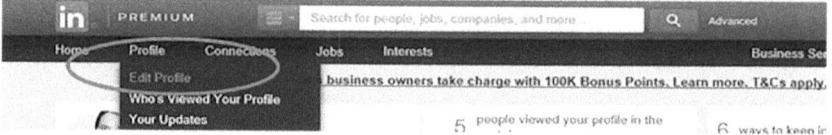

1. Click Edit Profile.
2. Click on Settings.
3. Click on Groups, Companies and Application.
4. Click on Set the frequency of emails.

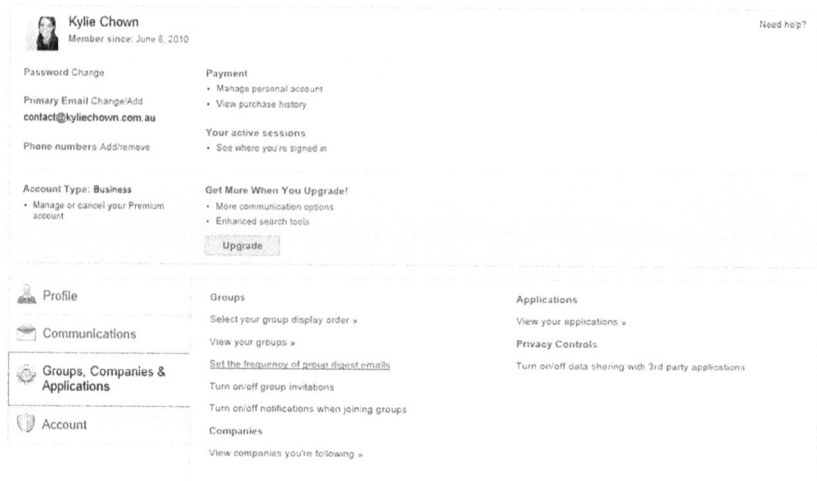

5. Select set the frequency of group digest emails
6. Select No Email, Daily Digest or Weekly Digest.

There are a couple of things to keep in mind with groups. They're the second-most important way to connect. The most important is introductions, and the third-most important is direct emails. Groups are also a great way for you to turn up in search results. You can have up to 50 groups.

How Do I Share an Update?

Once you have your shiny new profile ready to go, you can look at engaging with your network. One way to do this is to share an update.

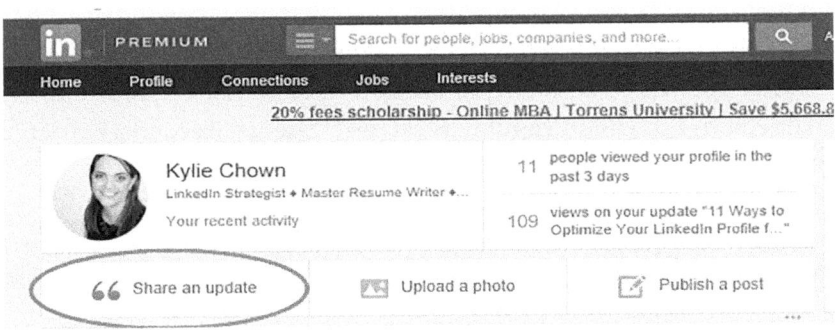

Action Steps to Share an Update

You can do this in one of two ways:

1. Click on the pencil icon and write a free-text update.
2. Click on the paper clip and attach a file.

You can share links to other articles in this section as well. You can do this by copying and pasting the URL in the "share an update" box.

LinkedIn is becoming a growth area for journalists to source information.

Have you seen the movie *Chef*? It is about a chef and his son. Dustin Hoffman is the crazy owner of the restaurant the chef works at. A food critic comes in and criticises the food. The chef gets really cranky. His son shows him how Twitter works, so the chef tweets to the food critics: "How dare you criticise my food?" The chef thought it was a personal message, however the message was actually public. The next morning, his son discovers a tsunami of comments on Twitter regarding the chef's tweet to the food critic. It had totally gone viral.

Jane woke one Sunday morning to discover that there had been a huge number of Twitter re-tweets and connection requests for her on LinkedIn overnight. The first thing she thought of was the movie, *Chef*. She thought, "Oh God. What have I done?", and frantically tried to work out what had happened overnight. What had actually happened was she'd recently written an article or a blog post on LinkedIn called "Seven Steps to Increase Your Likeability".

It was about rapport building and being able to connect with people. A journalist had picked it up in New York and re-framed it. She writes for "Business Insider Magazine", a big online business blog that has an Australian version as well. She had quoted a lot of what Jane had written in her own article, called "How to Be the Most Popular Person in the Office". She hyperlinked it back to her LinkedIn profile and said: "Jane Anderson, Personal Branding Strategist. She has recently written this article on LinkedIn about this." There were 8,500 views on LinkedIn.

Visibility and Consistency

One of the mistakes people often make with social media is thinking engagement is the goal. However, engagement is hard to achieve, so your goal should be visibility and consistency. People won't necessarily like everything you post. But the more we're seen, the more we're trusted and people get more of a feel for who you are.

Gihan Perera, author of *Fast, Flat and Free* and many other books about leveraging social media and branding, says it's a challenge to always get a return on investment with social media. However, if you can maintain your visibility on social media, even if it's just once a day, then it will give you enough brand equity to ask for what you want.

Rachel Bourke from Salespace wanted to use LinkedIn so she could be found by her ideal audience, be positioned correctly and have clients contact her via email or LinkedIn message.

Her profile was developed to:

- Support business-to-business (B2B) marketing.
- Nurture and strengthen relationships.
- Position herself to appeal to her ideal audience by tailoring language and keywords.
- Support branding and communication strategies.
- Curate, create and comment to support her expert positioning.
- Leverage search engine optimisation with industry keywords for B2B clients.

LinkedIn Strategy:

When we were approached by Rachel, her profile was a list of past roles and responsibilities. Her strategy focused on her future and included the following elements:

- Re-write a search engine optimised LinkedIn profile. The SEO was based on the keywords her ideal audience would use to find people such as her.
- Edit her summary and headline to reflect her business plan and targeted audience.
- Include testimonials from people her ideal audience can relate to.
- Compile content in her employment section to support her current business goals.
- Have a compelling call to action.
- Post search engine optimised articles to support her validation as an expert.
- Join and comment in groups to increase visibility and build credibility.

- Curate information of value to her audience.
- Share and promote business and industry events.
- Participate in coaching.

Rachel Bourke Initial Results

	Current score /10	Final score /10
Establish Your Profile		
1. Does your profile address the problems and fears of your ideal client?	5	10
2. Do you have a professional headshot?	10	10
3. Do you control updates clogging your inbox?	10	10
4. Is your profile fully search engine optimised in the title, summary, current role, skills and expertise, and does it include a vanity URL and contact details?	4	10
5. Are you well validated with recommendations and endorsements?	10	10
Total score /50	39	50
Engage Your Audience		
6. Do you like and comment professionally?	5	10
7. Do you create personalised scripts to connect professionally?	5	10
8. Do you leverage LinkedIn to support your face-to-face networks?	5	10
9. Do you curate content in a time-efficient and relevant manner?	5	10
10. Do you contribute to groups professionally?	5	10
Total score /50	25	50

Elevate Your Positioning		
11. Do you undertake advanced searches to find ideal connections?	5	10
12. Are you positioned effectively when being introduced to a potential client or contact?	5	10
13. Can you write a thought-leading post with a call to action to attract ideal clients?	0	10
14. Do you know how to write a compelling script to connect with ideal stakeholders via Connect or InMail, knowing the difference between the two?	5	10
Total score /40	15	40
Empower Your Team		
15. Can you maintain and troubleshoot your profile?	5	10
16. Do you know how to run your business page?	5	5
Total score /20	10	15
TOTAL SCORE /160	89	155

Results Immediately After Upload

Three-Monthly Tracking

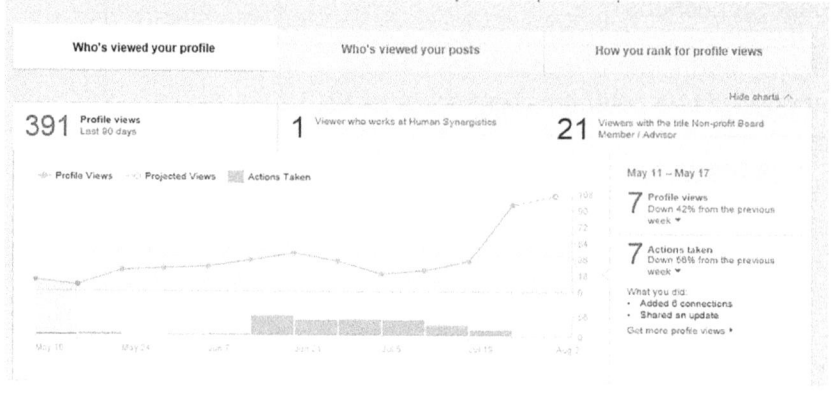

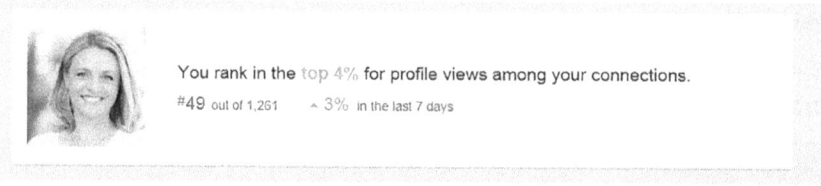

Impact on Posting

Posting was used to supports Rachel's positioning.

Date	View	Like	Comment
June 1, 2015	44	10	2
June 26, 2015	63	7	0
July 14, 2015	486	54	2
July 22, 2015	1419	96	12
July 24, 2015	4057	539	54

Date capture supports a 9120% increase in views on posts, 7600% increase in likes and a 2600% increase in comments (from lowest to highest viewed). Rachel's sales increased by more than 66% in the first quarter of her implementing the strategies from this book.

Scheduling Tools

Hootsuite is a tool you can use to schedule your posts. It means you don't have to sit down every morning posting content. You can allocate, say, half an hour every Friday afternoon to logging into Hootsuite, writing and scheduling posts. You can check out their website: www.hootsuite.com

Reflections and Actions

- Update your profile photo to mirror the type of clients you want to work with.
- Create a content plan based on the problems you solve for customers.
- Write a post at least monthly, if not fortnightly.
- Sign up for Scoop.it and hootsuite.com

Chapter 6

Connection

Brene Brown, author and expert in vulnerability, said in her TED talk: *"When you don't care what people think, you lose the opportunity for connection."*

In our experience, no matter the industry, we see the same issues with connecting. People are hesitant to connect because they:

- Are unsure how to approach or what to say.
- Can't override the default settings on devices.
- Are scared of pushing too hard, too quickly or not reading situations correctly.
- Don't optimise their profiles and are hard to find.
- Are worried people won't understand why they want to connect.

People need to earn the right to ask for a sale. For example, Jane has a friend who she has done some work with. Every day, this person puts up about 10 posts about herself and her business. Jane has had to actually turn off her feed because it's too much. She's not giving information.

Technology is moving fast. We try to keep you up to speed with some things that have changed. You might have noticed that people can start to post their own content if they have premium accounts, and those types of things. You see articles coming through that are a bit long, which is a tool called "pulse".

Connecting

When you conduct searches with particular words, your default will always be those that are first, second and third connections only.

Many years ago, Jane got divorced and her good friend Lisa recommended she go on a date with a guy she worked with called Travis. She kept saying that he was a nice guy, so Jane agreed. They met at a nice place in town but when Jane arrived, he had a backpack with him. She thought it was a bit odd, but went with it. They ordered an entrée and Jane asked Travis if he'd just come from the gym. He said "no"; he had brought his bag assuming the night would go well, and he laughed.

Hmm. Did he just say what she thought he said?

By this stage, Jane felt a bit awkward. As the entrée arrived, she asked: "So, what have you got in there?" He had fresh undies, his toothbrush, deodorant and a change of clothes. "Oh my goodness, he is actually serious!" Jane thought. Trying to remain calm, she laughed and said, "Well, that's brilliant because I had a key cut for you and the rent is due this week. I thought you might be able to help me out with that, too." At that point, she realised she had to wash her hair for the next day, so wrapped it up quickly, skipped the main meal and asked for the bill. It felt slimy and she couldn't get out of there quick enough. Sadly, he thought the date was amazing and called Jane the next day, saying it was such a shame she had to leave.

Have you felt like this when people have tried to sell to you and you haven't even met them? A common complaint we hear is: "Ewww, at least let me get to know you!"

Social selling and personal branding are a lot like dating. You need to let your audience get to know you. This helps your audience understand who you are, where you're coming from and to build trust. You can move slowly or quickly, but at least get a few dates in before you decide to try to move on to something more permanent. Otherwise, you look desperate. Self-promotion and marketing do not get the gig, whether it be the sale or the job. What they do create is awareness. Marketing is only one of the steps in the sequence of events required.

Winston Churchill once said: *"It is a mistake to try to look too far ahead. The chain of destiny can only be grasped one link at a time."*

Make it easy for your audience to get to know you. You can do this through sharing ideas, articles, curating content and your own thought leadership. That way, when you want to progress the relationship, they know who you are and if they like you or not. It takes time to build trust.

When approaching people, what you're looking for is common ground. Remember to personalise your connection requests because nobody does it. You've only got 300 characters to work with.

The next step is for that person to get used to your newsfeed and visibility so they get to know you. We're not trying to go home with the backpack on the first date. All we want to do is connect and say "hi". Let them know the reason you are connecting is because you have something in common with them. The goal is to maintain your visibility so people can get to know you.

Let People Get to Know You

Help people get to know you. People buy when they're ready, so you need to increase the amount of touch points to build trust. It's like a bank account. Imagine that you have a bank account with minus $50. You have to build it up past zero and get it into the black.

Robert Cialdini, best-selling author of *Influence, the Psychology of Persuasion* was the one who said that you need five to seven touch points to influence and persuade someone to do something. To do this, you need to know what you want and who you help. You need daily visibility and you need to be writing your own content weekly.

InMail

You might have noticed there is an opportunity called InMail. InMail gives you a few more characters, allowing you to provide more information.

Search

LinkedIn allows you to search a keyword string and put constraints around it. For example, "CEO":

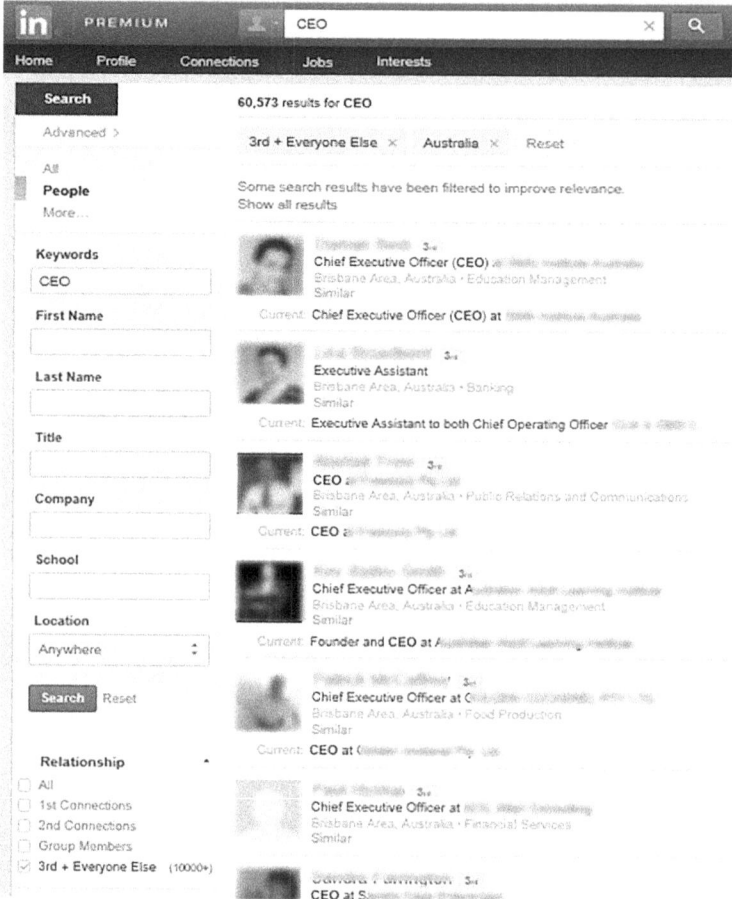

Connections

Once you have your profile set up, you can start inviting new connections. People who you can connect with include:

- Current colleagues
- Past colleagues
- Clients
- People from networking events

- Industry leaders
- Experts in the field
- Class members of past studies
- People who have viewed your profile

NOTE: LinkedIn currently caps the maximum number of connections at 30,000.

Action Steps: Adding a New Connection

To invite a new connection to your LinkedIn network:

1. Search for their name in the search box in the top field.
2. If the person isn't in the drop-down list, select the magnifying glass for all options.
3. If you have a long list, you can use the advanced search functions on the left-hand side to reduce the search criteria.
4. Once you have found who you are looking for, you can either Connect, Save, Get Introduced, Send InMail, Share or Find References.

Top Tip: It is easier to do this on a desktop computer. It is difficult to customise your connection requirements on a mobile device. Take the time to do it professionally – you only have one chance at a first impression.

From here, you can connect directly or make an approach. To connect, select the connect option and compete the form.

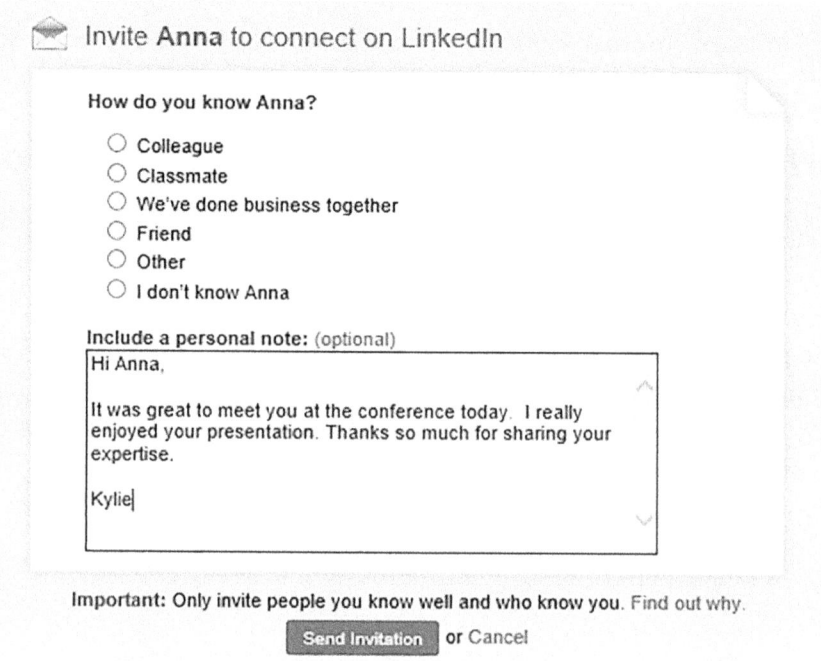

The other option for adding connections is to use the import feature.

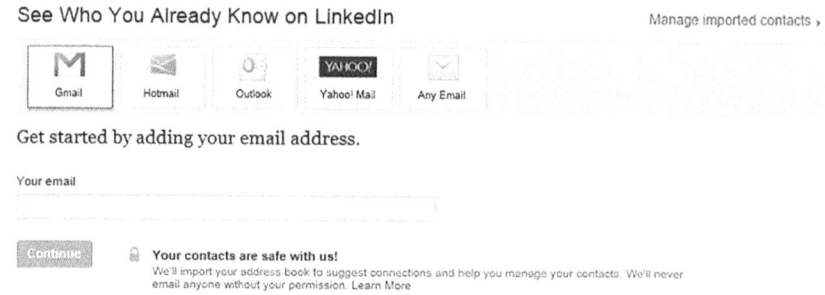

Be careful if you import your connections this way. We do not recommend this as you do not have control over who you are connecting with.

Action Steps

1. Go to the Contacts and select Add Connection.
2. Enter your email address and password and click continue. From here, you can choose who you would like to connect to.

Top Tip: This will only work if the person you are connecting with is using the same email address for their LinkedIn account.

When connecting, always personalise the connection. Not many people do this, so it is a great way to stand out. If you have met them at an event or conference, mention that it was great to meet them, highlight something about them and ask to connect.

Once you have added a connection, you can keep notes, set a reminder, remember how you met and tag them.

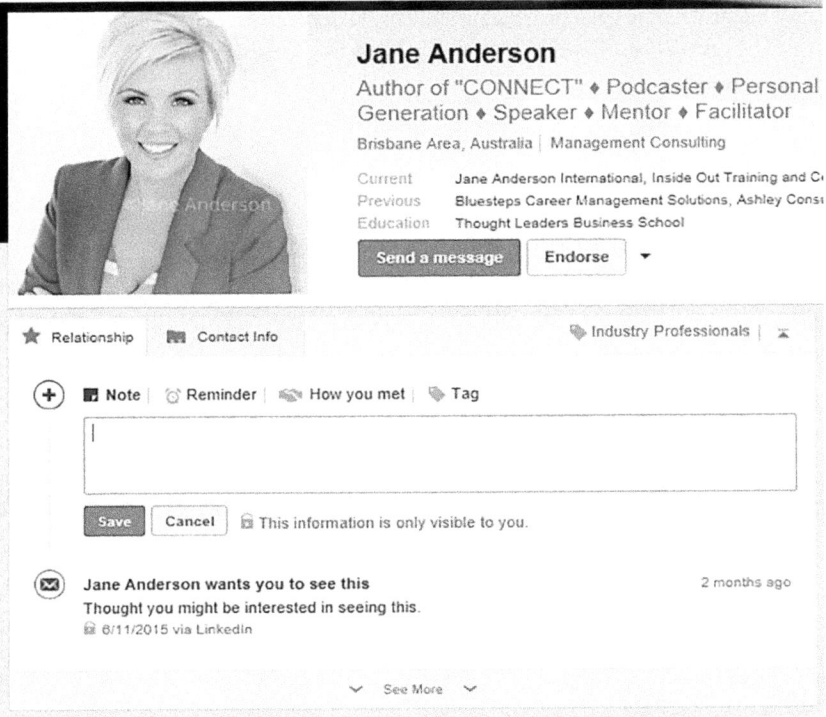

You can set a reminder that is only visible to yourself. This will appear on your contacts page as an action item.

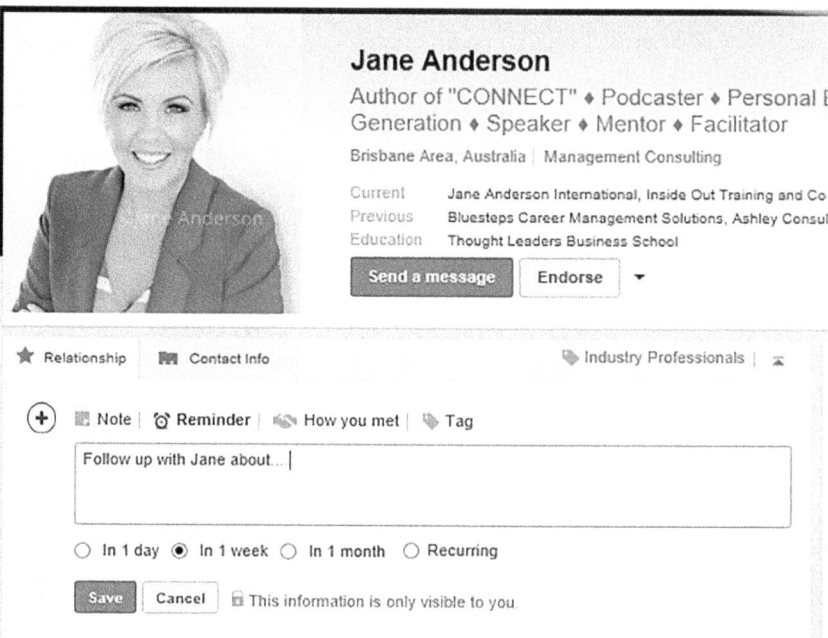

Accepting Connection Requests

Remember that you don't need to accept all connection requests. There have been instances of fake LinkedIn accounts, so it is important to validate the request. You might like to look at whether you have any connections in common. If you can't determine why they have connected with you, you can always email them to ask!

When someone does connect with you, it is always a good idea to send them a quick message. Something along the lines of: "Thanks so much for connecting, Mark. Looks like you are doing some great work at (company name). I find most people who connect with me need help with their LinkedIn profile. Is there anything I can help you with?"

Again, not many people do this, so if you do, you will stand out.

When Others Connect With You

When people connect with you, be curious. Don't just accept it and soldier on with your mission to find new clients; they're right in front of you, even if you can't understand why they are connecting with you. Your profile is a similar to a shop front, so when customers "walk in", say hello and see if you can help.

If they connect with you, don't just accept and ignore it. Our research tells us that about 50% of people connecting with you are connecting because they want help – if not now, at some stage in the future.

To illustrate, Phillip connected with somebody on Friday afternoon. He asked them if he could be of any help, and by Monday he had received a $100,000 proposal. On Tuesday, they called him in for a meeting, and he was also put forward for further work within the organisation.

People want to move quickly. Help them do this by saying, "Thank you very much for connecting." Ask them if you can be of any help. Ask them if they would like to receive your newsletter. Offer tips and tricks. Make notes of your connections, use tags and use reminders if you need to follow them up.

Taking Notes

You can record notes specific to each connection, set reminders (that will sit on the top of your contacts page), and record how you met.

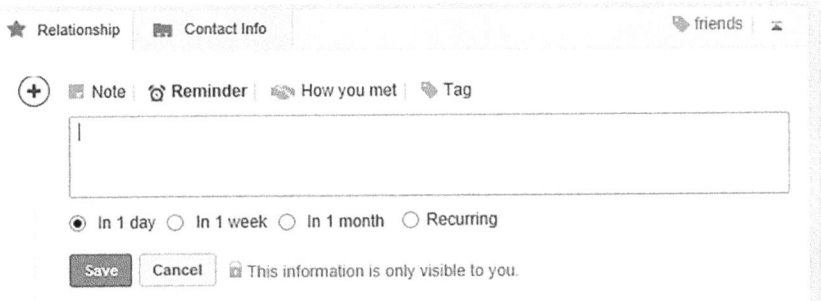

Tagging

You can tag your LinkedIn connections so you can group, sort and organise them for searches and messages. As the maximum amount of connections you can message at one time is 50, it is recommended that you do not have more than 50 connections with the same tag. One way to work around this is to have sub-tags. For example, you might have HR Managers, HR Managers 1, HR Managers 2, HR Managers 3 or more targeted groups, such as HR Managers Finance Sector, HR Managers Health Sector, HR Managers Retail Sector, etc. Only you can see your tags and you can create up to 200 tags.

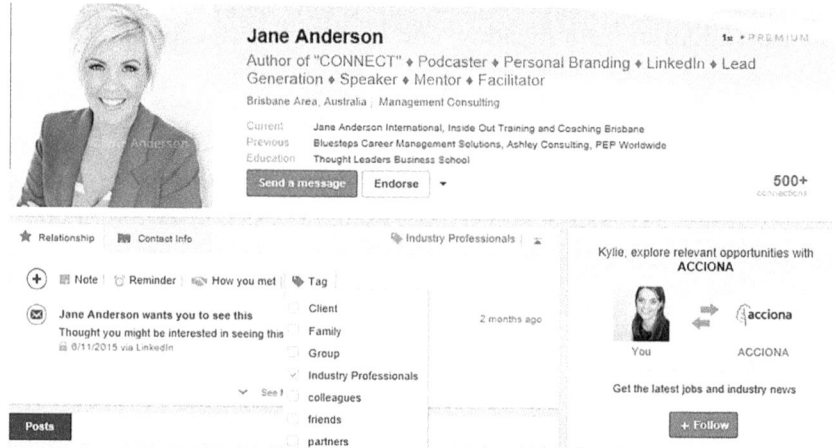

Action Steps

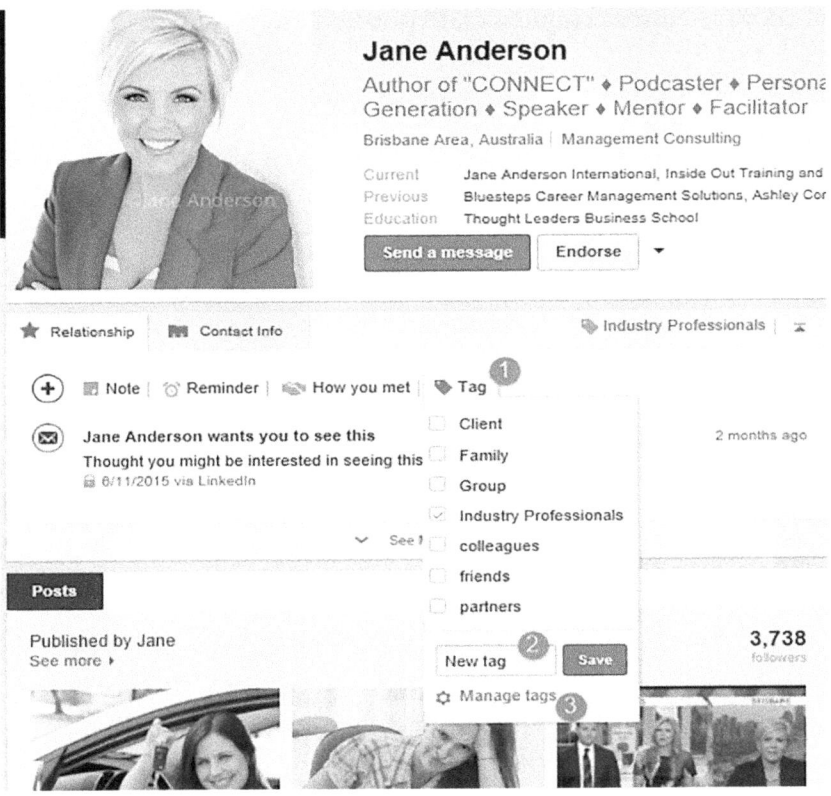

1. Select Tags.
2. Select a Tag or create a new one.
3. Manage tags.

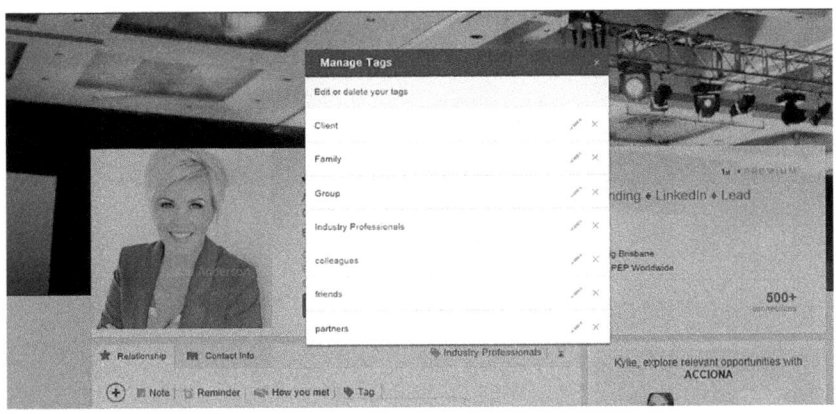

Exporting Your Connection Data

You can export your connection data from LinkedIn into a spreadsheet. Only the full name, email address, current employer and position are exported.

To do this:

1. Move your cursor over Connections at the top of your homepage and select Keep in Touch.

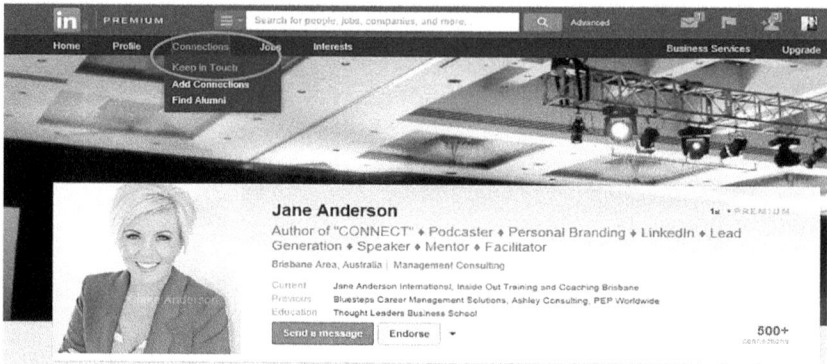

2. Click the Settings icon near the top right to reach the Contact Settings page.

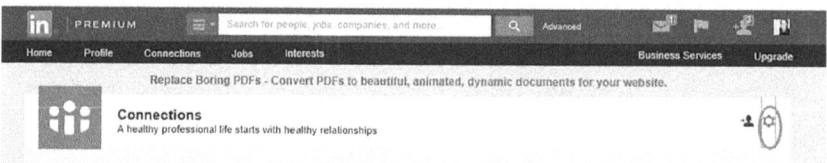

3. Under Advanced Settings on the right, click Export LinkedIn Connections.

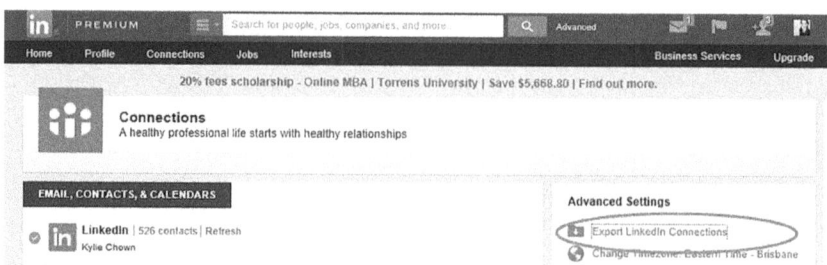

122 | CONNECT: Leverage Your LinkedIn Profile for Business Growth and Lead Generation

4. Enter the security verification text if prompted and then click Continue.
5. Click Export.
6. Save the file somewhere you can easily find it, such as your computer's desktop.

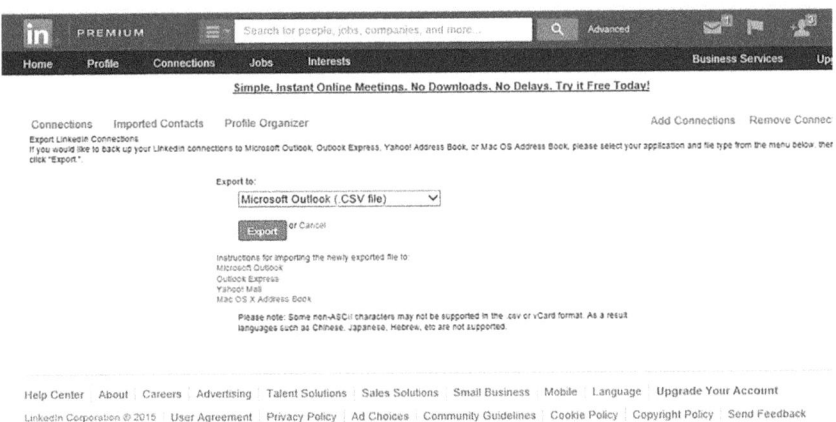

7. Open the file and print (optional).

Top Tip: It's a good idea to back up your connections on a regular basis in case anything happens to your profile – for example, if it gets hacked.

Sorting Connections

You can sort and filter connections by recent activity, first name, surname and newest. To filter your connections, click the filter option above the contacts.

Keep an Eye on Who Likes Your Comments the Most

Our other little tip for you is to keep an eye on who looks at your stuff. For example, Jane has a connection on LinkedIn who frequently comments and likes her articles and posts. Jane approached him and said, "I'm very grateful that you have been sharing your insights and your comments and liking my articles. Is there anything I can do for you? Do you want any feedback on your profile? Is there something I can help you with?" He replied, "Actually, I'd love to get feedback on this." Jane's connection has done a lot to advance her thought leadership. Keep an eye out for those people who are liking what you're doing. They can be a good source of business development. As

Seth Godin would say, they can help you build a tribe. They're people who buy into what you do regularly.

Asking For an Offer in Line With the Equity You've Built

Imagine you're driving along and see one of those inflatable men outside a furniture store. Then, you see a newspaper ad that says the store is having a big sale. You also hear an ad on the radio saying, "Get down to the furniture store." You've got all these messages about the furniture sale coming at you. People need at least five messages before they think, "Oh! Geez, I think we need a new lounge."

It's the same deal with social selling. It complements the other selling and marketing tools we use. The key is that we don't want to go too fast on the first date. We want to help people get to know us first and gain positioning.

Scripts

When you go to a particular profile, you've got a few options. You can set reminders. When you go onto a profile, you can make notes for yourself on how you met, and you can also create any tags to a profile.

You have two wording options when you go to approach someone. One is dependent on whether you're connected already, but the other is not.

The first option is if you're not already connected. It might be that you are a member of the same group. You might have someone in common. You might be interested in the same thing. You could say: *"Hi (their name), I noticed that you're …"* or, *"I notice that we work in this particular industry …"* or, *"I notice that …"*

You want to validate the person. You want to show that you've paid attention to what they're saying and what they do, so you're looking for common ground.

"I help organisations like yours," or, *"My role is …"* or, *"What we have in common is …"*

A great way to position yourself is through a positive first impression, so you need to personalise it. Make the person feel important and show what you have in common.

The second wording option is for when you are already connected. This wording is for when you want to progress the relationship. If you're already connected and you've been posting, sharing, curating and commenting, you may feel as though you have built enough brand equity so you can think, "Right now, I feel like I'm ready to talk to this person."

You might have used a reminder on the person's profile to follow up a week after you've connected with them. You're trying to progress the connection and give them more information. For example:

"Hi, I noticed that you're the employee relations manager for this particular union or organisation. I help organisations such as yours in this capacity."

"I recently delivered a speech at an organisation that is similar to yours. Would it be helpful if I sent you some information?"

Be mindful of your wording when you're reaching out to people, and always connect at a personal level, such as: *"I thought I'd follow up. Would it be helpful if I popped in and said hi?"*

Altogether, it looks something like this:

"Hi (the person's name), I noticed that you're the employee relations manager for this particular union or organisation. I help organisations like yours in this capacity. I recently delivered a speech at this organisation that is similar to yours. Would it be helpful if I sent you some information?"

Additional Sample Scripts

For Someone Offering to Connect With You:

Hi [Name]

Thanks so much for your connection request, I appreciate you reaching out. It looks like you're doing some great work in the [name] industry, congratulations on getting Manager of the Year! Well done.

Is there anything I can do to help? If not that's okay, just thought I'd ask.

Kind regards,

[Your name]

Sales Script if Already Connected

Hi Bill,

I noticed that you're ...

I help people/organisations like yours in ...

For example, I recently delivered ...

I'd love to send you my [video/whitepaper/first chapter of my book]. Is [address] the best one to send it to?

Kind regards,

[Your name]

Sales Script if Not Already Connected

Hi Bill,

My name is [name] and I noticed that you [are a member of the same group; know someone in common; have the same interest; work in same industry].

I help people/organisations like yours [in what capacity], so I thought I'd offer to connect and send you a free whitepaper on the challenges in the industry for [their position title].

Is this the correct email address to send it to? email@email.com.au

If so, just say yes and I can get it to you today.

[Your name]

Followed Up By

Send via email:

Hi Bill,

Hope you're well. I thought I'd see if you found the whitepaper helpful.

I'm currently delivering a training/coaching/facilitation program addressing the issues covered, such as [problem]. If this is something that might be helpful for you, I'd love to chat to you about it.

I can do the following times next week if any of these work:

- Date and time
- Date and time
- Date and time

I look forward to hearing from you.

Your sincerely,

[Your name]

Connecting Through Groups

You can conduct a search on the groups you might like to join. If you're interested in a closed group, you will have to be approved to join. Some are open groups and you can become part of that group instantly. You can be a member of up to 50 groups. If you do become a member of a group, you might want to set up a rule in Outlook so that the group's updates go to a reading list, which you read once a week.

Leveraging Your Profile for Events

Before you attend a conference, check whether the organisers are using a hashtag on Twitter and keep an eye on who is posting in the Twitter feed. Try to find them on LinkedIn and connect there. This way, you will have done half the work on connecting with attendees and finding out what you've got in common before the conference. Bear in mind that you will turn up in their search results, too.

Dropping them a line before the event is a great way of positioning yourself to meet them face to face:

"Hi, I noticed that you're attending this event that's coming up in a few weeks. I'd love to catch up with you. I just thought I'd introduce myself here so I could keep an eye out for you on the day. I hope that's okay with you."

It's also a great idea to follow up and connect with people on LinkedIn within 24 hours of the event. Don't just put their details into your Salesforce system; make a personalised experience for them. Drop them a line to say, "It was fantastic to meet you." Write the personal connection rather than use the default wording.

Always send messages from your desktop with a personal introduction. Mobile phones and iPads don't allow you to do personalise a connection. Always look for ways you can add your personal touch.

Reciprocity means that you're more likely to get back if you give first. It's as though people have a bank account in their minds: "Have I given more? Am I being used here? Have I given too much? Am I in debit or credit?" Look for ways of giving first because you're more likely to receive what you're looking for. For example: "I really want to acknowledge you at this point to say keep up the great work!"

Reminders

With some profiles, you'll see there are notes where you can set reminders and make comments about how you met. You can even set email reminders to make sure you follow up with someone. You can put tags on them as well. The main consideration with your approach is to look for what you have in common. Look for referrals, join the same groups and comment on articles.

Disconnecting

Jane had been connected with a particular person for a while when she noticed that he had started to post many times every day, filling up her newsfeed and notifications. The tsunami of self-promotion led to her decision to disconnect with him. He may have thought he was adding value, but Jane didn't see this in any of his posts – it felt like they were all about him and how good he thought he was.

People won't know if you disconnect with them or ignore their connection request until they go to your profile.

Follows

Follows are different to groups. They are for influencers, and you can follow anybody's posts now. If you look at Richard Branson for example, you'll notice it's difficult to connect with him on LinkedIn. If you know Richard, you can connect, but otherwise most people will follow him. He has almost seven million followers.

You'll notice he has an influencer logo on his profile. This means that LinkedIn have specifically chosen him to be an influencer. You cannot decide to become one yourself.

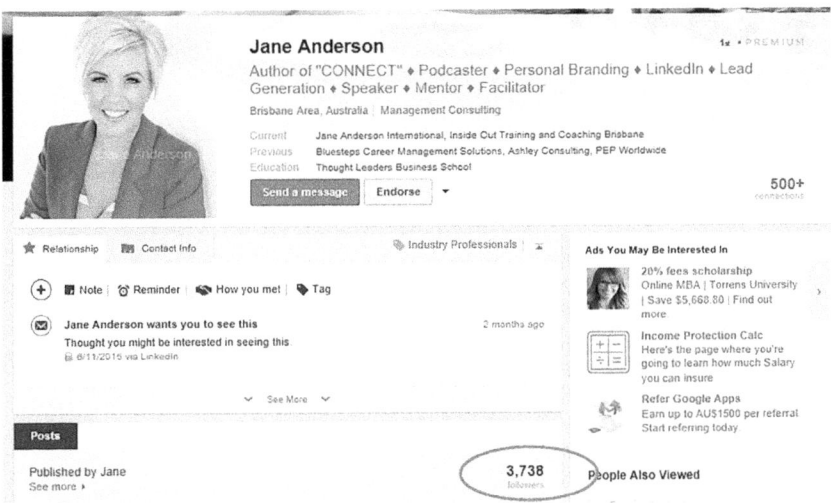

Reflections and Actions

- Write scripts you can use when connecting with others. Save them as a Word document to copy and paste when connecting with others.
- Export your connections at least once per month
- Search for those who help you the most and make offers to connect using your script.

Chapter 7

Organisational LinkedIn Strategy

Do you have a LinkedIn strategy for your organisation? How do you know it's working?

Everybody has a different role in your organisation, but remember it's not just about dealing with customers. It's about dealing with suppliers, the community, removing roadblocks, validation, and building trust within your business.

It's a bit like buying a car. You do your research and look around. You ask: "Can this car be trusted? Am I getting a reliable vehicle? Is it going to do what I need it to do?"

People are savvy. They're not stupid. They will do their research. The best thing about having a LinkedIn profile for your organisation is that it's a great way to beat the competition if you're a small player in a big industry.

Other reasons why an organisation might have a presence on LinkedIn, particularly for its leaders, include:

- 75% of job seekers validate managers and CEOs on LinkedIn when they apply for jobs.
- 60% of a buying decision is made before you've even heard from a customer. They may have already decided on buying the product; they just need someone to talk to.

We recently worked with a medium-sized organisation in the health insurance industry. It's a small player in a big industry. After helping the organisation with personal LinkedIn profiles for its team members, it was able to beat its competition in Google searches.

Seth Godin, one of the world's leading marketing authorities, describes in his book *Linchpins* those people in organisations who are highly leveraged and have a high impact on the business and its success. In your organisation, these may not just be sales people, but technical experts or those who have high visibility outside the organisation.

When deciding on who needs to have their LinkedIn profile written, you might like to think about those people in your organisation who are linchpins. Do you have team members who speak at conferences and events or connect with different people across your industry? It's important to make sure these people have a well-written profile. You need to consider their roles, write with a purpose and include their personalities.

If you are a school principal, your profile is much like a CEO's, and you need to think about your profile as part of the school community and less about you. The parents of your students will often be on LinkedIn, so it's a great way to show your professionalism and another touch point to market your school.

The overall strategy and design for an organization's LinkedIn program like peeling layers of an onion off. There are different layers and each person has different purposes in their role in that layer. It will also depend on the closeness to the customer

This model shows the steps to building your profile, whether you're an individual or a business owner looking to bring LinkedIn into your organisation:

LinkedIn Strategy for Individuals and Organisations

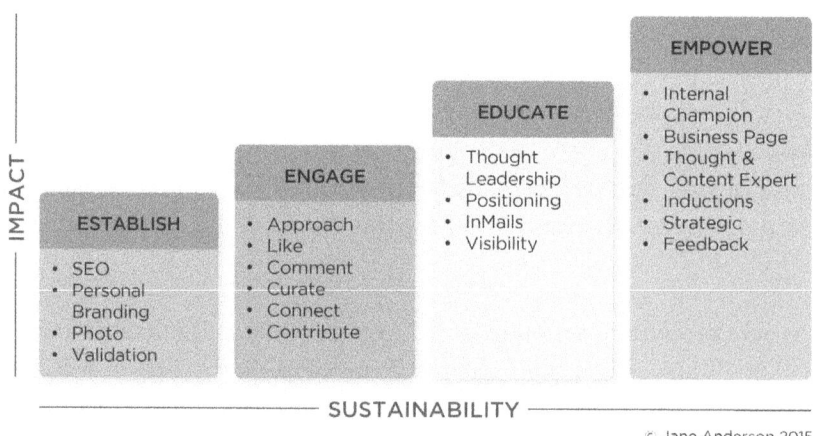

Establish: The first step is to consider your profile. Do you even need one? If you have a profile, how professional is it and how do you want it to serve you? You profile works for you 24/7, so it needs to align with your goals, support your face-to-face activity and define what you're trying to achieve. You need to make sure your team's profiles are fully search engine optimised, have a professional presence with a professional photo, and are well validated.

Engage: You need to teach your team members how to engage online – how to like things, how to comment and curate content, how to connect with other people, what to say and what scripts to use. They need to learn how to contribute to conversations and understand the etiquette of contributing to forums and groups. Are they comfortable sharing content? Are they aware of the impact of liking and commenting on content and how that supports your goals? Do they personalise their introductions and connect with others in a way that is meaningful and achieves results? Do they add value to their audience or are they spamming them?

Educate: The third level is about teaching people how to educate and this involves their positioning as thought leaders. They must be clear about their content strategy. What is the purpose? What do they want to be known for? This is about your team members becoming thought leaders and teaching them about thought leadership.

Your team needs to know how to write connection requests and InMails to clients and customers to initiate conversations. Visibility is about making sure your team is top of mind so that when people need help, your team members are who people think of.

How are you educating your audience to elevate your positioning? Is your content strategic enough? Are you known for what you want to be known for? How often are you seen in the average person's feed? Are you top of mind for referrals?

Empower: At this level, you're thinking about your business strategy and how LinkedIn fits with your goals at an organisational level. It's not just about having a profile written. Your team members own their profiles. How do you educate them to make the most of their profile? Do you have a LinkedIn policy in place? How do you on-board them? Do you have an exit strategy? How are you measuring success? This is where we're working with marketing and communications teams to make LinkedIn sustainable within organisations. This is about having an internal champion who is trained in how to get a LinkedIn strategy to work.

Checklists for Senior Management LinkedIn Profiles

If you're a CEO, here is a checklist with some questions to help you determine if your LinkedIn profile is working for you and where you need to focus your efforts.

	Current score /10	Final score /10
Establish Your Profile		
1. Does your profile address the problems and fears of your ideal client?		
2. Do you have a professional headshot?		
3. Do you control updates clogging your inbox?		
4. Is your profile fully search engine optimised in the title, summary, current role, skills and expertise, and does it include a vanity URL?		
5. Are you and your business well validated with recommendations and endorsements?		
Total score /50		
Engage Your Audience		
6. Do you like and comment professionally?		
7. Do you personalise your connection request scripts professionally?		
8. Do you leverage LinkedIn to support your face-to-face networks?		
9. Do you curate content in a time-efficient and relevant manner?		
10. Do you contribute to groups professionally?		
Total score /50		

Elevate Your Positioning		
11. Do you undertake advanced searches to find ideal connections?		
12. Are you positioned effectively when being introduced to a new connection?		
13. Can you clearly represent your organisation, vision and purpose?		
14. Do you know how to connect with ideal stakeholders via Connect or InMail?		
15. Do you write posts that position you as a brand ambassador?		
Total score /50		
Empower Your Team		
16. Do you have a LinkedIn expert on your team with the knowledge to maintain or troubleshoot your profile?		
Total score /10		
TOTAL SCORE /160		

If you're a sales or marketing manager, here is a checklist with some questions to help you determine if your LinkedIn profile is working for you and where you need to focus your efforts.

	Current score /10	Final score /10
Establish Your Profile		
1. Does your team have a LinkedIn profile as a brand ambassador attracting ideal clients instead of recruiters?		
2. Do your team members have professional headshots?		
3. Does your team control updates from clogging inboxes?		
4. Do your team members' profiles include a search engine optimised title, summary, current role, skills and expertise, and vanity URL?		
5. Is your team supported with leaders who have strong profiles?		
Total score /50		
Engage Your Audience		
6. Does your team like and comment professionally?		
7. Does your team personalise scripts to connect professionally?		
8. Does your team leverage LinkedIn to support face-to-face networks?		
9. Does your team curate content in a time-efficient and relevant manner?		
10. Does your team contribute to groups professionally to drive enquiries?		
Total score /50		

Elevate Your Positioning		
11. Does your team undertake advanced searches to find ideal clients?		
12. Is your team positioned effectively when being introduced to potential contacts on LinkedIn?		
13. Can your team write a customer-centric post defining customer problems and with a call to action to attract ideal clients?		
14. Does your team know when to connect with ideal clients via Connect or InMail and the difference between the two?		
15. Does your team maintain visibility aligned with your sales strategy?		
Total score /50		
Empower Your Team		
16. Do you have an internal LinkedIn expert to advise, troubleshoot and maintain profiles?		
17. Does your marketing and communications team run the business page effectively?		
18. Is there an internal thought leader and content expert who knows how to write posts and can advise the team on posting their own articles on LinkedIn to drive sales?		
19. Do you educate new employees on managing their professional presence online?		
20. Is there a champion who can talk at a strategic level on leveraging LinkedIn for the organisation?		
Total score /50		
TOTAL SCORE /200		

If you're a school principal, here is a checklist with some questions to help you determine if your LinkedIn profile is working for you and where you need to focus your efforts.

	Current score /10	Final score /10
Establish Your Profile		
1. Do you have a LinkedIn profile that is reflective of your school's marketing and branding, and less about you?		
2. Do you have a professional headshot?		
3. Do you control updates clogging your inbox?		
4. Does your profile include a search engine optimised title, summary, current role, skills and expertise, and a vanity URL?		
5. Are you and your school well validated with testimonials and endorsements in your profile?		
Total score /50		
Engage Your Audience		
6. Do you like and comment professionally?		
7. Do you connect professionally with others using personalised scripts?		
8. Do you leverage LinkedIn to support your face-to-face networks?		
9. Do you curate content in a time-efficient and relevant manner?		
10. Do you contribute to groups professionally?		
Total score /50		

Elevate Your Positioning		
11. Do you undertake advanced searches to find ideal connections?		
12. Are you positioned effectively when being introduced to a new connection?		
13. Do you clearly represent your school's vision and purpose?		
14. Do you connect with ideal stakeholders via Connect or In Mail, knowing when to use one and not the other?		
15. Do you know how to write posts that position your school to parents of prospective students?		
Total score /50		
Empower Your Team		
16. Do you have a LinkedIn expert on your team with the knowledge to maintain or troubleshoot your profile?		
Total score /10		
TOTAL SCORE /160		

CEO and Principal Profiles

After working with a large number of CEOs and their profiles, many say they don't have the time to waste on LinkedIn and are still doing the old ways of business. However, they say they do want to grow their businesses as their markets have become tougher. Changing customer demands and technology means their competition is getting in front of their clients more quickly and they need to gain ground.

As mentioned in Chapter 1, many CEOs have a number of fears about LinkedIn:

Loss of Talent

CEOs worry that well-written LinkedIn profiles will lead to recruiters poaching their organisation's talent. If that happens, it means the profile has been written incorrectly. The LinkedIn profile writing strategy for a team member versus a job seeker is very different. It is a different process, with a different result. If the profile is written based on what the organisation wants to achieve, then it won't appear in talent pools and it will be clear to a recruiter that the team member is not looking for a job.

Looking Stupid

Many clients we work with have a fear of looking stupid or not being able to manage their profile successfully. They are also concerned that they won't know how to manage the situation if they post something online that people disagree with.

Competitors

Others are concerned that the competition may use LinkedIn to see what they're doing. "What if they try to steal my clients? How do I protect my connections, my clients and myself?"

BLACK-BELT LINKEDIN PROFILE FOR A CEO

LEVEL	ACTIVITY	LEVERAGE
6	Influence	100% +
5	Magnet	75%
4	Organisation	50%
3	Future-focused	25%
2	Obituary	0%
1	Profile	-10%

A leader's LinkedIn profile, especially a CEO's or principal's profile, is all about leverage.

Level 1: Profile: This is the lowest level, where you may have had a profile created for you. You have no idea how you turned up on LinkedIn, you just simply woke up one day and you had a profile. The amount of leverage you have here is about minus 10% of what's possible. It's actually repelling people from your business because they don't understand it. There's no information, so your profile is not doing anything for you. In fact, it's having a negative impact because it makes your competition look much better.

Level 2: Obituary: At the next level, your profile is written as though it's an obituary. It's written about the past; it's about your previous jobs, your study, and all those types of things. The amount of leverage you have at this level is zero. It's only leveraging you as an employee and you are far more likely to have recruiters contacting you. The leveraging is zero because it's not inspiring. It doesn't motivate others to want to work for you, it doesn't connect with potential customers or potential talent, and it doesn't open any doors for you.

Level 3: Future Focused: When your profile is future focussed, it has been written strategically, but it's been written about your own future, not the company's. You will receive more interest from recruiters and hiring managers. You haven't thought about how people are contacting you. Your profile's leverage is about a quarter of what's possible. It makes you look good, but it doesn't serve the business and it doesn't serve the growth of the company.

Level 4: Organisation: At this level, your profile has been written more about the organisation. You've provided some information about the organisation's careers pages, you're leveraging plugins from websites, you've possibly added product disclosure statements, and you're more focussed on the type of talent that works in the business. However, your profile is not particularly compelling. Its leverage is about 50% of what is possible.

Level 5: Magnet: At the next level, your profile is like a magnet. It is focused on the organisation, but it takes the reader into the future and into what the organisation is trying to achieve. It has full search engine optimisation, so if somebody tries to find the types of services your business offers, you turn up in their search results. It also means you're not having to search for good talent; you're starting to draw them in, and potential opportunities are coming to you, such as strategic partnerships. The leverage your profile has is about 75% of what's possible.

Level 6: Influence: This is a profile that has influence. At this level, you have 100%-plus of the leverage that's possible. Your profile inspires people to want to work for your organisation. It creates influence with stakeholders and strategic partners. It influences customers – we know that two-thirds of customers will make a decision about employees based on their perception of the CEO. You, as CEO, are making it very clear that it's not all about you; it's about the organisation. It's also about your influence in the community, so you're leveraging things such as your corporate social responsibility. It serves as a strong touch point to help you get access to people, such as investors, who will help the business grow. You're leveraging your LinkedIn profile for the benefit of the organisation, and it's making you look good.

How to Build a CEO or Principal's LinkedIn Profile

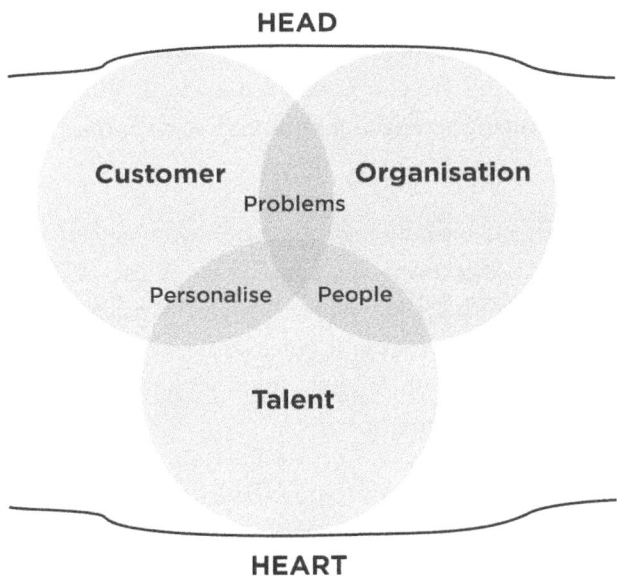

If you're building a CEO profile on LinkedIn, there are three factors you need to ensure it includes:

Customer: You must identify the customers you work with, their problems and the challenges they face, and even their fears. The content you share and the plug-ins you include need to have leverage and appeal to potential customers by connecting with their problems and fears. The profile must be fully search engine optimised, so a customer can find you based on their problem.

Organisation: A good CEO profile means it is more about the identity of the organisation and less about you. It's about the kind of business you have, addressing questions such as: "Is it a good place to work? Does it contribute to the community? What is its corporate social responsibility?" It also shows what the organisation is trying to achieve: "Our goal is to be the leader in X industry," or, "Our goal is to be Australia's favourite provider in X, or to be a world leader in X." It needs to be aspirational and it needs to highlight not just the organisation's goals, but its vision and values.

Talent: The profile needs to show the type of person who would be a good fit as an employee of the organisation. You could include turnover rates of the business. You could even provide a testimonial from a team member. This is particularly important if you're on a talent drive. Research shows that almost 75% of potential employees review the profiles of an organisation's leaders when applying for an advertised position at that organisation.

Underscoring these factors are three important points. Your profile needs to connect with the **problems** your customers have. It must be **personalised**, so it needs to make the connection between how we make a difference in the world and the customer. Finally, it also must also make a connection with the type of **people** who work at your organisation.

People can make very head-based decisions when they're considering working for an employer. They focus on questions such as: "What is the organisation trying to do? What is it trying to achieve? What's its vision? What's its purpose? Does it have a good name in the industry? What outcomes is it getting? Am I going to be paid?" All these are head-based questions around whether the person is going to work with you or whether they're going to be your customer.

Fifty per cent of the population makes logic-based decisions. The other 50% makes heart-based decisions. Those heart-based decisions focus on questions such as: "How am I going to feel when I work with you as an employee? How am I going to feel when I get to use your products or your services?" Your profile needs to connect at a personal and heart-based level because if you only focus on outcomes, results and tasks, you will only sell and leverage your profile to half the population. Here is an example of a CEO's summary:

Sample Company X provides equipment solutions, including excavators, mini excavators, hydraulic rock breakers, wheeled excavators, demolition excavators, wheel loaders, skid Steer loaders, materials handling excavators, compaction rollers and drill rigs.

We service a range of industries, including quarry and mining, civil, pipelining, plumbing, landscaping, forestry, demolition, materials handling and public works. Our clients (based in Australia, NZ and PNG) include Boral, Aurizon, Queensland Rail, Incitec Pivot, OneSteel, Xstrata, BGC, Leighton Holdings, Rio Tinto and Hansen.

We support our clients by supplying cost-effective sales and rental solutions for construction projects, helping them become more profitable, effective and sustainable, as well as enabling them with the latest technologies. In addition, we support them to maintain their assets by offering a competitive after-sales service function.

With more than 12 years' experience with Sample Company X, our team has:

♦ Doubled the Hyundai national support footprint, supporting both our customers and Australian jobs.
♦ Improved quality-control techniques through the pre-delivery process to reduce warranty and downtime from manufacturing defects by 90%.
♦ Provided parts and service support, which includes a 99% fill rate within five days on all parts, factory-trained personnel and a quarterly published parts pricing.

More recently, we have:

♦ Achieved high engagement scores for our team. We're a great place to work, we have low staff turnover and many have been in the business for more than 10 years.
♦ We give our staff one day per year to work in a charity of their choice. Many say this is one of the reasons why they love working with us and it gives them a sense of contribution to the world.
♦ We regularly have team development days and are committed to each team member achieving their potential.

Reflections and Actions

- Who looks at my profile? (i.e. customers, partners, talent)
- What is the vision for my organisation?
- What customer problems do we solve?
- Why is our organisation a great place to work?
- How do we undertake our corporate social responsibility?

Chapter 8

Metrics vs Results

Peter Drucker, world-leading management consultant, once said: "What's measured improves."

In 1988, an Australian woman called Leisa Campbell took the world by storm. She was an Australian body builder from Victoria. She won Miss Australia, Miss World and Miss Universe. Leisa travelled the world, competing and living in Europe and the US. She was before her time and even by today's standards is still considered one of, if not the, best body builders in the world.

When she was training, many things were measured that still are now, such as skin folds, fat percentage and weight. However, Leisa said she focused on something not all competitors valued. It was a diary of how she felt each day. She kept notes on her body's reaction to foods, sleep and training. Today, as a personal trainer for more than 25 years, she asks her clients to keep a diary as well. She says people pay too much attention to a whole lot of metrics that don't have enough leverage. They are just the results. The diary is what has leverage. In his book *The Power of Habit*, Charles Duhigg calls habits such as the diary keystone habits. These are every-day habits or leverage points that create big results.

Your LinkedIn profile is the same. It's easy to focus on the various LinkedIn metrics available, such as the All-Star rating, the new SSI (Social Selling Index), your profile's ranking, and the number of people who have viewed your profile and taken action. These metrics can motivate you to undertake more activities and stay on the site for longer.

In isolation, these metrics appear valuable and people tend to spend a lot of time trying to achieve an All-Star rating and an SSI score of 100%. However, as a result of the work we have done with clients, we have found that there are a number of other metrics that create the best results.

LinkedIn Metrics	Profile Keystone Metrics
All-Star rating	Search engine optimisation
Social Selling Index score	First four seconds
% viewed in your networks	Original thought leadership & curation
Post views, likes and comments	What action people take when looking at your profile
500+ connections	Effective scripts to connect with ideal clients
Connections	Ask if you can help connections who reach out to you

Why These Metrics Matter

- **Search engine optimisation:** It's important that you are easily found. LinkedIn is a search engine and there is someone out there trying to find you. Make it easy for them!

- **First four seconds:** When someone lands on your profile, you only have four seconds to "wow" them. If you don't, it will take a lot of work to impress them and motivate them to want to work with you. Your first four seconds needs to link to your future, not your past, otherwise you will only receive more of what you've already had.

- **Original thought leadership and curation:** Curation should comprise about 80% of your posts. Ideally, your original thought leadership (i.e. writing a post as opposed to sharing an update) should comprise about 20%.

- **What action people take when looking at your profile:** When people look at your profile, they should feel compelled to connect with you. If you have enough of the right content, the right connections and the right information for your first four seconds, people will be more likely to connect with you. This metric is important to review, however, it depends on the context of the views. For example, if you have a smaller amount of views but a high amount of clicks through to your profile, this is a good sign. It's all relative to what you're putting out there. This is the area of your profile that tells you this:

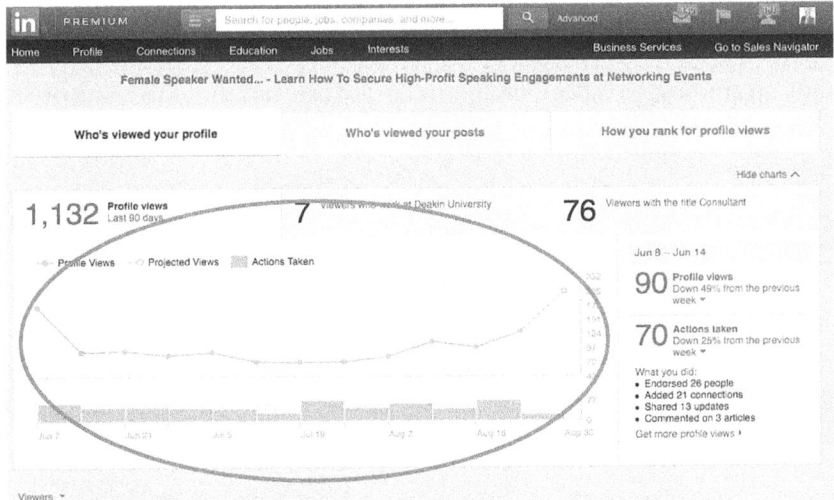

- **Effective scripts to connect with ideal clients:** Clients don't just magically appear. With effective scripting, you can maximise your chances of engaging with the right people. With the wrong scripting, you will repel them!

Why These Metrics are Less Important

- **All-Star rating:** The purpose of this rating is to encourage you to complete your profile. Yes, you certainly do want to complete it; however, if the content doesn't position you for your future, your profile will only give you more of what you've received in the past.

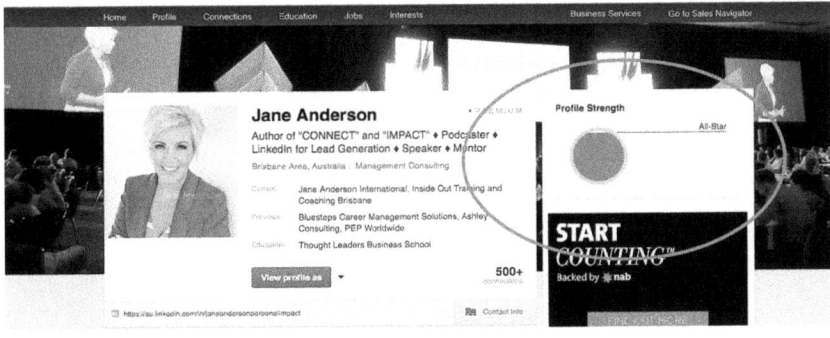

- **Social Selling Index:** The Social Selling Index is an indicator of how well your profile is leveraged as a sales tool. It is impossible to get a score above 85 without upgrading to Sales Navigator. A lot can be done on your profile to not only lift your score, but to leverage it for social selling before you upgrade to Sales Navigator.

- **Post views, likes and comments:** Just because you get a lot of views or likes doesn't mean you're generating leads. It also doesn't mean that you're doing something wrong. What matters is if your content speaks to your tribe, its problems and aligns with your goals.

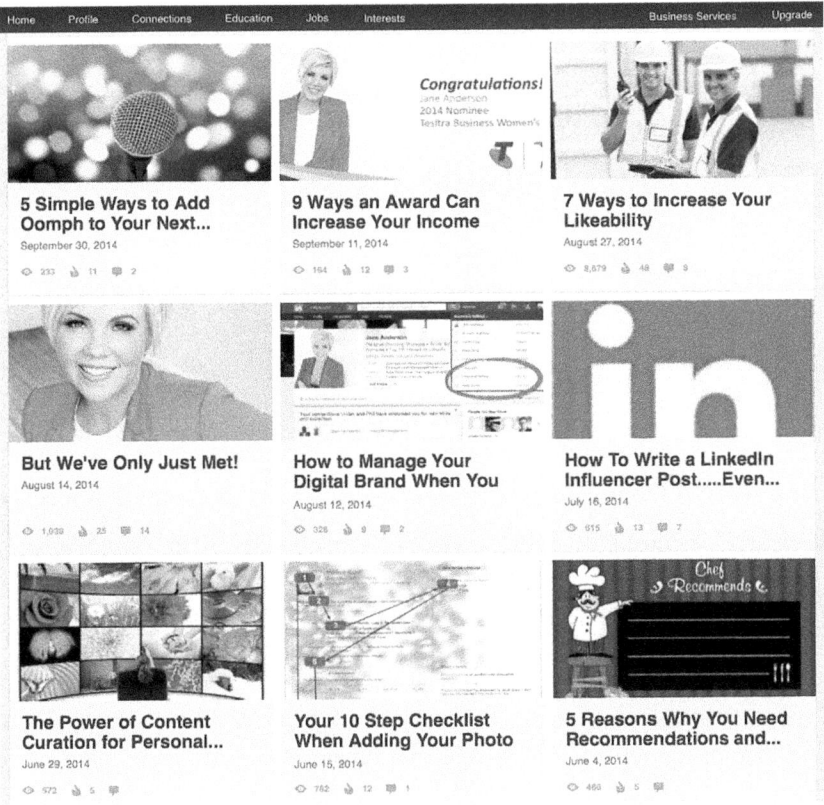

- **500+ Connections:** Having a large number of connections doesn't mean you're selling a lot. Yes, it may mean you turn up in search results, but the first question you need to ask is: "Is this in line with the goals I'm trying to achieve?" If not, then you need to make sure you're building the right tribe!

- **% viewed in your networks:** This measurement is based on the words in your profile and the connections you have. In other words, you could rank highly if you have a high number of keywords but a low number of people in your network use the same keywords. You could also have a low rank if you have a lot of connections in the industry who use the same keywords. It pays to regularly check your Boolean search, rather than be overly concerned about this score.

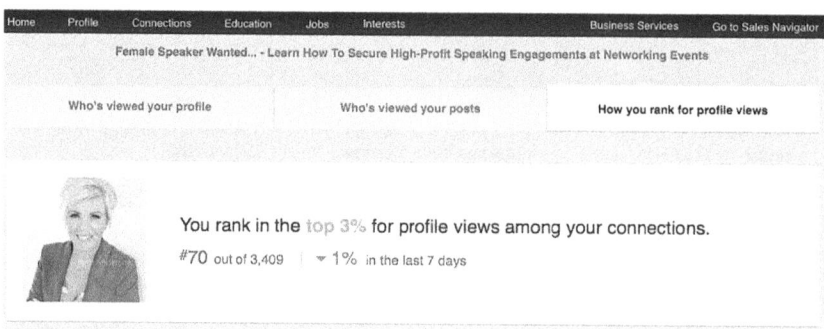

- **Connections:** The amount of connections you have certainly increases the amount of search results you're in. However, if you're connecting with everyone and not personalising the experience for them, it can seem a bit "smash and grab". Taking the time to personalise your connections takes extra effort, but it does pay off.

Overall, your metrics need to move potential clients into your sales meetings. If you focus on likes and comments, then you're not encouraging them to become clients.

Reflections and Actions

- Test your search engine optimisation by undertaking a Boolean search. Make any changes to keywords.
- Update your profile to create your "first four seconds".
- Personalise your interactions.
- Share your thinking through posts and curation.

Chapter 9

LinkedIn Groups

By now, you may be aware that LinkedIn offers you to be a member of a group. In fact, you can be a member of up to 50 groups. There are thousands of different groups. Some are closed groups, where you need to be approved by the manager of the group. Others are open groups, which means anyone can join.

The purpose of groups is to connect you with others who are like-minded or in the same industry as you. It's where your customers hang out.

Some of the most common questions we are asked by clients relate to being a member of and running a group.

Benefits of Being in a Group

- It expands your ability to be returned in search results. You will turn up in someone's search result if you're a first, second, third-level connection, and also if you're in the same group.
- It allows you to contribute to discussions and share your area of expertise.
- It can give you a direct line of communication with your ideal audience.
- Your contribution to the group sends a clear message to connections about your expertise, interests and passions.
- A group can help you find people in your local area with similar interests to you, particularly if it's a location-based group. This is especially helpful if you are new to your region.
- It increases your profile views. This is achieved by increasing your search results and people's curiosity when they see you making comments in the group.
- Groups build your knowledge and expertise.

Disadvantages of Being in a Group

- You receive updates in your inbox daily or weekly, summarising what has been happening in the group. If you're a member of 50 groups, this means a lot of email landing in your inbox.
- It may mean people pigeonhole you based on their perception of the group.

- There is limited ability to include personal branding in responses. You cannot include the same level of formatting that you can in a personal email, such as hyperlinks and a signature block, for example.

Benefits of Running a Group

- It positions you as a leader in the industry and you effectively become the "go-to person". It also allows you to include your website address in the group description.
- You have access to a responsive audience. A group owner has influence in the group and can direct the group's direction.
- It gives you visibility across your areas of expertise, and you are the "first to hear" what's happening.
- When a member joins a group, the group details and logo will be displayed on their profile. This increases the group's visibility.

Disadvantages of Running a Group

- It can be incredibly time consuming. However, there are features that can reduce this. These include an automated welcome message to new members, and the ability to create sub-groups that allow easier targeting.
- Once you start a group, you cannot close it so you need to be committed!
- There is limited analytics and return on investment data. It is hard to gain a tangible measure of running a group.

Running a group might be helpful for you when you have a community of like-minded people who are open to sharing. It would not be helpful if the group has a high potential for conflict and negative engagement.

Top Tips for Starting a Group

- Have a clear purpose for the group.
- Complete all the required fields and ensure all members know the group's guidelines and expectations. Setting clear expectations will help you manage a situation where a member does not comply.
- Make sure members know what to expect from you. For example, will you be checking in daily or weekly? You could consider co-managing the group to reduce the workload. Expectations management is key.
- Use the automation features to reduce manual workload.
- Maintain engagement by contributing topics for discussion and providing positive feedback to All-Star group members.

How to Start a Group

When you are logged into your profile:

1. Under Interests, click Groups.

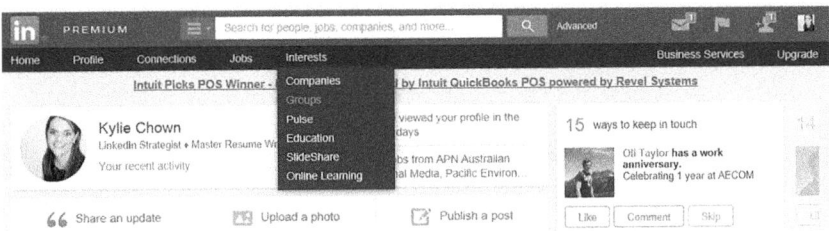

2. Click Create A Group.

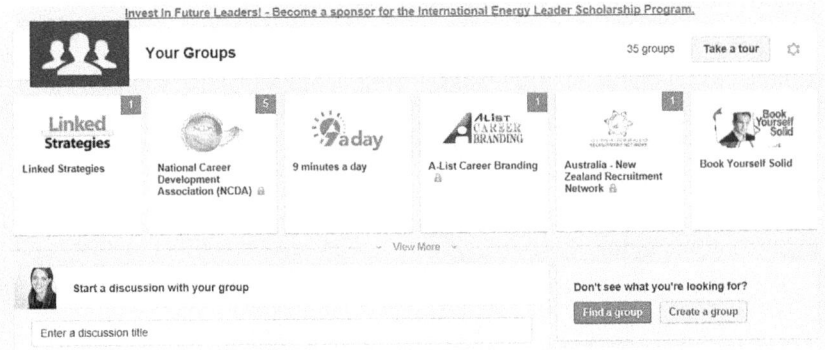

Reflections and Actions

- Does your ideal customer hang out on LinkedIn?
- What value will the group give to members?
- What will a group allow you to do that a standard profile doesn't?

Chapter 10

Company Pages

Basketball legend Michael Jordan once said: "Talent wins games, but teamwork and intelligence win championships."

Kylie recently worked with a client who was setting up her own business. The client wanted to set up both a personal profile and a company page, and asked what she should do first.

Your personal LinkedIn profile is an extension of your personal network and brand. It's a way for you to connect on a personal level online. A business page is slightly different. While personal profiles have connections, company pages have followers.

Simply wanting people to follow your business instead of connecting with you is counter-productive when networking and growing your business. People want to connect with you because you're you. It's similar to when you're at an event – you introduce yourself as you, not your company.

However, LinkedIn research indicates that members are 50% more likely to purchase from a company they engage with on LinkedIn. Furthermore, nearly 80% of LinkedIn members want to connect with companies in their lives. In other words, members aren't looking for once-off help. They want to connect and partner for the longer term. Your business page and personal page allow this to happen.

Benefits of Having a Company Page

- Elevates the quality of talent applying for a role. Potential employees will review your company page, so make sure it reflects your organisational values.
- Leverage company visual branding by including images and logos. A company page is also a great place to share videos.
- Add specific products and services and launch new products and services.
- Share updates and provide a collection of information team members can easily share within their own personal networks. This allows the company to engage with followers.
- Can be used when individuals link their personal profile to the company in their Employment History. The logo and correct name is on their own profile.

- Allows you to plugin to other media. This means you can link your LinkedIn company page to the company website and add a follow button to other websites.
- Supports paid advertising as being able to be defined as a precise audience.
- Provides analytics and data.
- Supports SEO by including keywords.
- You can drive traffic to your LinkedIn company page by including a follow button on your company website.
- Provides a way for your competitors to follow your business rather than you sharing your content and connections with them and putting your business at risk.

Some Disadvantages Include

- Needs an allocated page manager with a process in place for hand-over if the person leaves the organisation.
- Ongoing maintenance is required to ensure relevance.

An important point to note is that if you attempt to set up a company as a personal profile, your profile will be removed by LinkedIn. This means you lose all your connections and will have to start all over again, as LinkedIn ultimately owns your connections, not you. So don't risk it!

To Add a Company Page

1. Click over Interests and select Companies.
2. Click Create in the Create a Company Page box.
3. Enter your company's official name and your work email address.
4. Click Continue and enter your company information.

You do have the ability to see who is following your page if you wish:

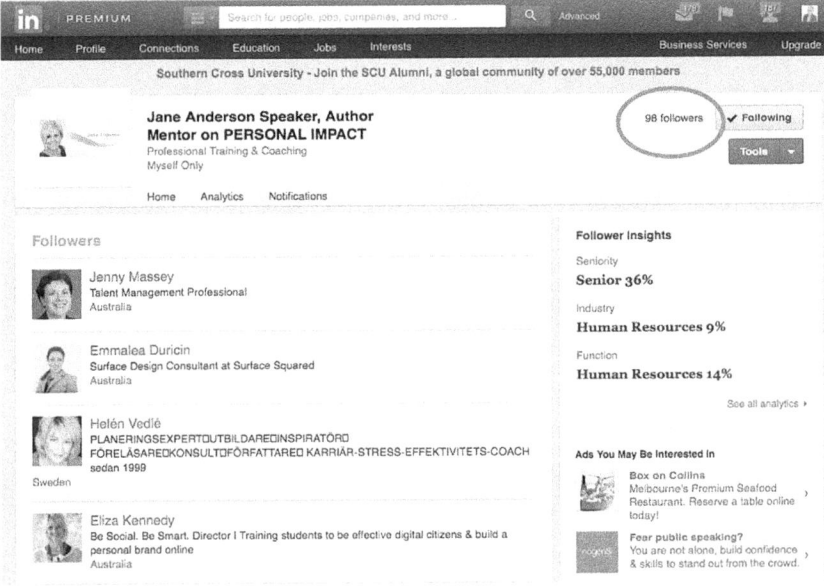

Reflections and Actions

- Do I not want people connecting with me and often due to my position? (i.e. if you're the CEO)
- Do I have a team of experts that differentiate our business and can contribute their thought leadership on a business page?
- Am I growing the business and recruiting in the future, or do I currently have positions advertised on other websites?
- Do I plan to run ads on LinkedIn?
- Do I have competitors who could be looking to capitalise on my network?
- Do I have the resources to manage both pages?

Chapter 11

FAQs and Resources

Should I Have a Premium Account?

Like anything that offers a free and paid version, the product will generally develop to support paid users. Paid LinkedIn accounts offer advantages in how you present on LinkedIn and what you can find.

From our experience, LinkedIn has become less generous with the features of a basic account. It has taken some features that were basic and put them in premium. The main difference you'll find is the amount of InMails you can use. If you have a free account, you may notice you can't connect with someone without approaching them with an InMail, in which case you pay once-off fee. If you can do everything you need to, a free account is great. Our suggestion is to use that.

As of July 2015, the accounts included:

Basic (Free) Account

A basic account is for anyone who wants to create and maintain a professional profile online. You can:

1. Build your professional identity on the web.
2. Build and maintain a large, trusted professional network.
3. Find and reconnect with colleagues and classmates.
4. Request and provide recommendations.
5. Request up to five introductions at a time.
6. Search for and view profiles of other LinkedIn members.
7. Receive unlimited InMail messages.
8. View 100 results per search.
9. Save up to three searches and get weekly alerts on those searches.

Premium Accounts

LinkedIn offers premium account options for job seekers, sales and talent professionals, as well as general professionals who want to get more out of LinkedIn. If you have a free account and want to upgrade, you can compare the account types described below.

1. Land your dream job with **Job Seeker**.
2. Unlock sales opportunities with **Sales Navigator**.
3. Find and hire talent with **Recruiter Lite**.
4. Power your professional life with **Business Plus**.

Top Tip: From time to time, LinkedIn may offer you a trial of a paid account. This is a great opportunity to test an account and see if it is for you.

Can I Get Some Efficiency With Outlook to Manage LinkedIn?

If you are getting digests and feeds from LinkedIn, you can manage them with rules. To do this in Microsoft Outlook:

1. Make sure you are on the home tab. Click Rules. Create Rule.

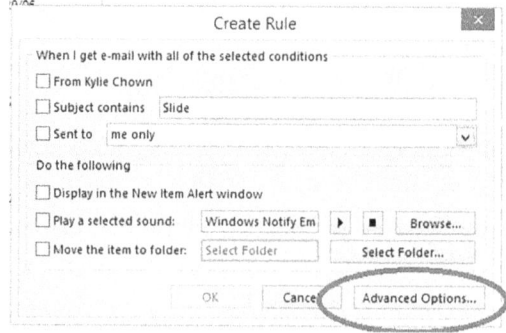

2. Click Advanced Options.

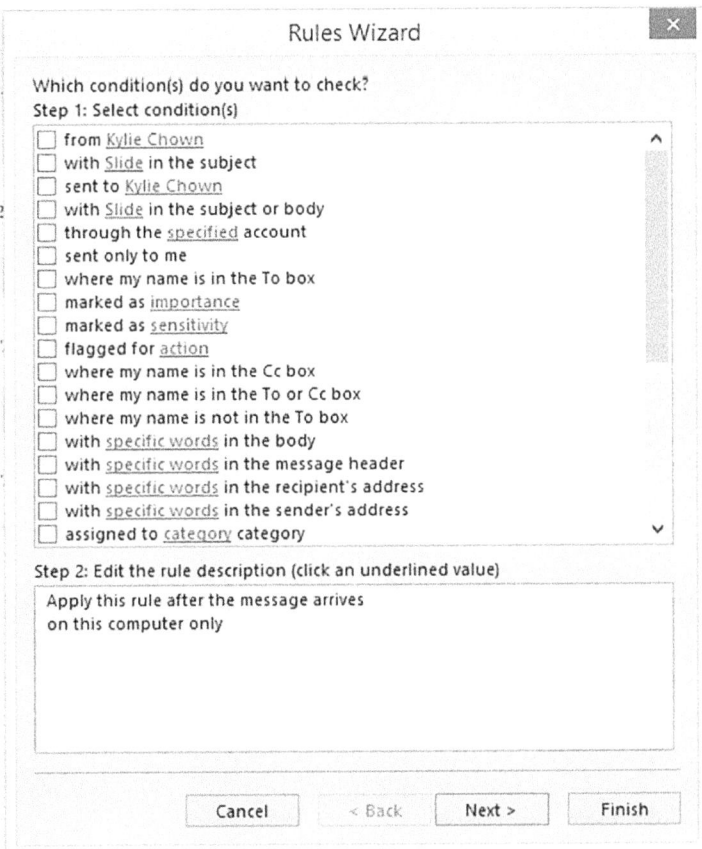

3. Select your criteria options.

What About Profile Maintenance?

Your LinkedIn profile is not static and can be updated to align with your current goals and objectives. Updates can include:

- Any changes to your client testimonials.
- A review of your plans and goals each quarter. When you're business planning, look at what your goals are for the next 12 months and then what your goals are for the next 90 days.
- Adding or changing your plug-ins.
- Adding projects and moving them up in the profile.

If you are a thought leader, you can align your profile around your current cluster and business owners can align their profile around their 30/60/90-day plans.

How Long Do I Need to Spend on LinkedIn to See a Result?

Apart from your initial set up and strategy planning, you should be able to manage your LinkedIn profile in seven minutes a day.

Some things you can do in seven minutes include:

- Review curated content and share.
- Like a post and make a comment.
- Search and connect with your ideal audience.
- Facilitate an introduction via a connection.
- Export your connections.
- Write scripts.
- Make a list of people to contact.

Or you can combine your seven minutes into a weekly allocation of 35 minutes and:

- Write a blog post.
- Create a comprehensive strategy with a targeted outcome.
- Compile new scripts and communication structures.

I Am a Business. Who Owns My Team Members' Profiles?

A LinkedIn profile is owned by the specific staff member. This includes the content, connections and headshot. Companies and businesses may consider their social media policy and seek their own independent, legal advice.

How Do I Get My Team to Engage on LinkedIn?

In our experience, there are a number of strategies that can be used to maximise engagement. Resistance from team members can be presented in a number of ways that include: "I don't: have time for this / know how to do this / want to look silly."

To address your team's concerns, focus on the following areas:

Education: Educating team members on the benefit and value of LinkedIn will help them overcome their fear. If you can show your team how LinkedIn can make their job easier, they will be more likely to support the initiative.

Technical support: Providing the team with content to share and strategies to support the development of their own content is beneficial. This may include an internal champion who provides team members with advice when required.

Incentivise: Collaborating in a team environment supports a group approach and an "everyone else" is doing it mentality. Successful businesses have made LinkedIn management a key performance indicator or criteria for internal awards. Ongoing positive reinforcement will further support All-Star users.

In our experience, not everyone may be willing to jump in, but once they see the rewards LinkedIn offers, they will be more likely to get involved.

How Do I Know it is Working? What is the ROI?

There are a couple of measures you can use to gauge the success of your LinkedIn strategy. If your profile is effective, you should see an increase in the quality of connection requests you receive.

Additional measures include:

- Who has viewed your profile and are they your ideal audience?
- What action was taken by people who looked at your profile?
- How did they find you?
- What changes are there in LinkedIn search results and Google search results?

How Do I Export My Contacts ?

Depending on your role, we advise clients to export their contacts every 30-90 days.

To export your contacts:

1. Move your cursor over Connections at the top of your home page and select Keep in Touch.

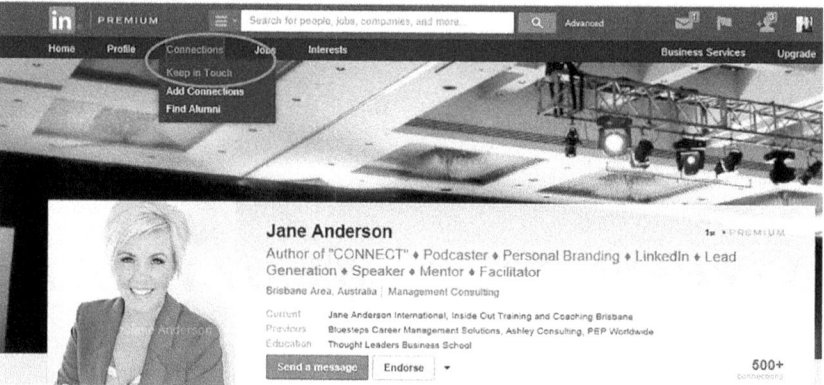

2. Click the Settings icon near the top right to reach the Contact Settings page.

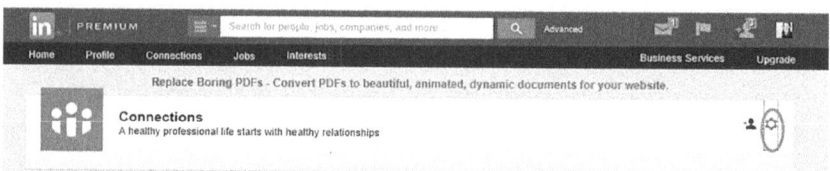

3. Under Advanced Settings on the right, click Export LinkedIn Connections.

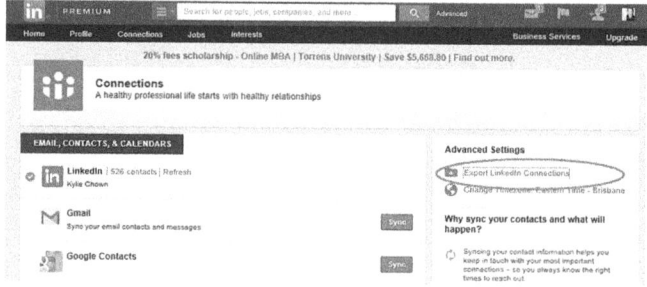

4. Enter the security verification text if prompted and click Continue.
5. Click Export.
6. Save the file where you can easily find it, such as on your computer's desktop.

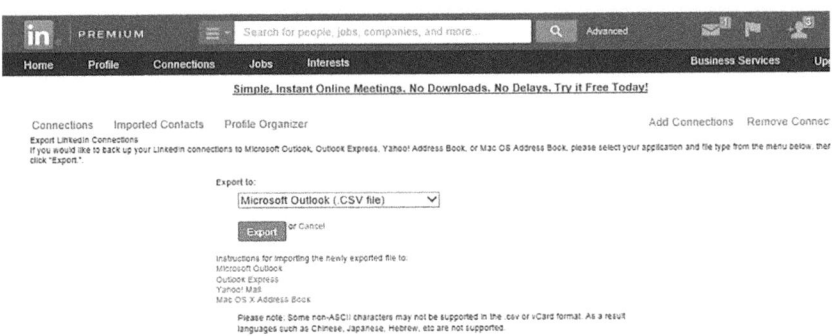

7. Open the file and print (optional).

By choosing Outlook, a file will be exported in a format that can be opened in Excel.

Should I Connect With Everyone?

It depends on what your goal is with LinkedIn. By having a goal, you can decide who you will connect with. For example, if you want to develop your network, you might be more open to accepting requests than if you are just starting out.

What Happens if Someone Connects With Me and I Don't Know Who They Are or Don't Want to Connect?

If you receive a connection request and you are not sure why, you can always send them a message, such as: "Thanks for requesting to connect. Generally, when people connect with me, it is because they would like assistance with ABC. Can you please let me know how you would like me to help?"

What Am I Missing if I Don't Set Up a LinkedIn Profile?

By actively investing your time in developing a quality LinkedIn profile, you take control of your account and mitigate the risk of others setting up a fake account under your name.

What if I Start a New Role?

You can easily add a new role under your employment history. To do this, once you are logged into your profile:

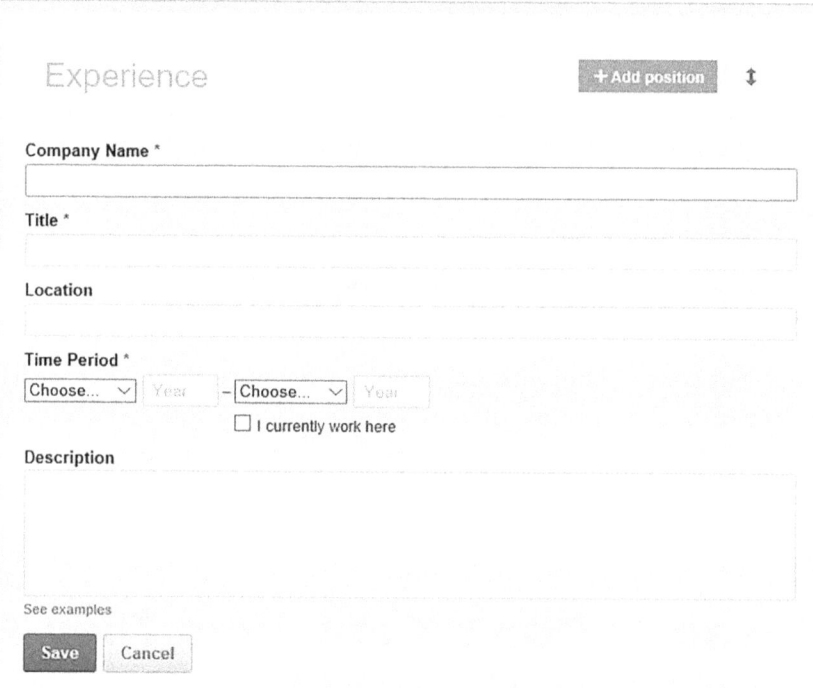

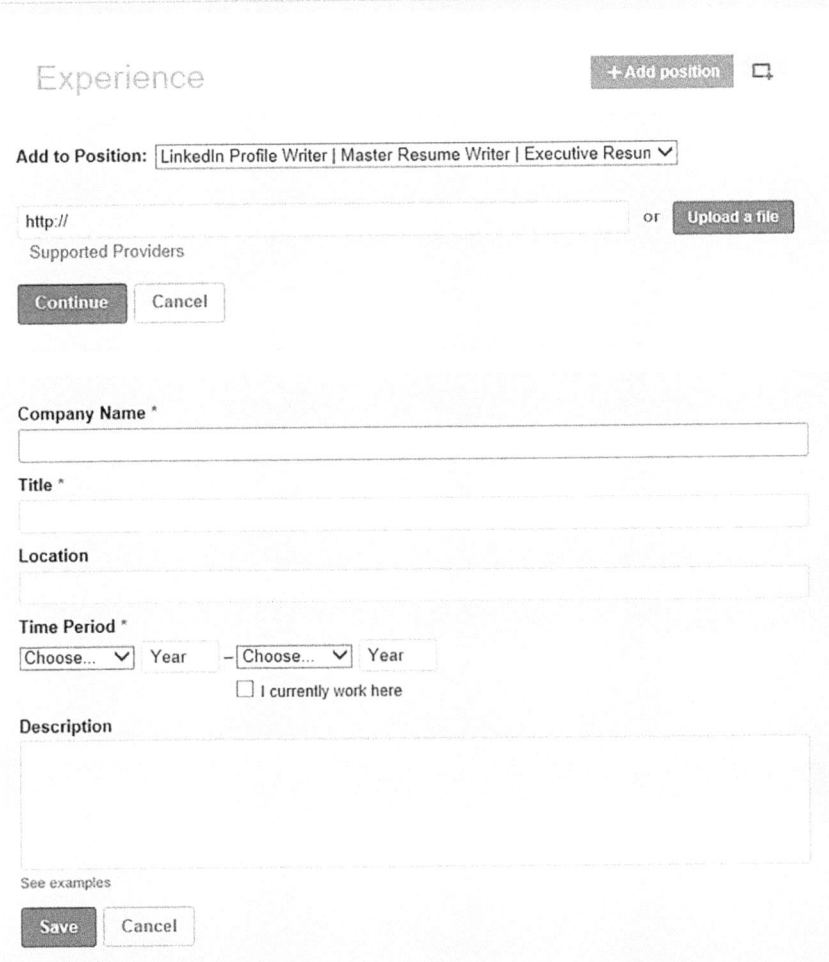

You can also upload your summary to capture the new direction.

How Do I Get a Banner?

This can be hard to get right as it's an awkward shape that runs around the header. If you are a thought leader, your banner is in a hero speaking shot. Books can be hard to position across the banner unless you create a mosaic or tiled effect. The banner has lots of "boom" factor for your first four seconds, so use it well! If in doubt, get assistance from a graphic designer.

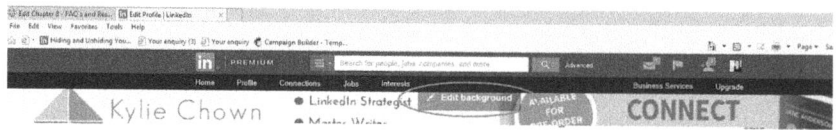

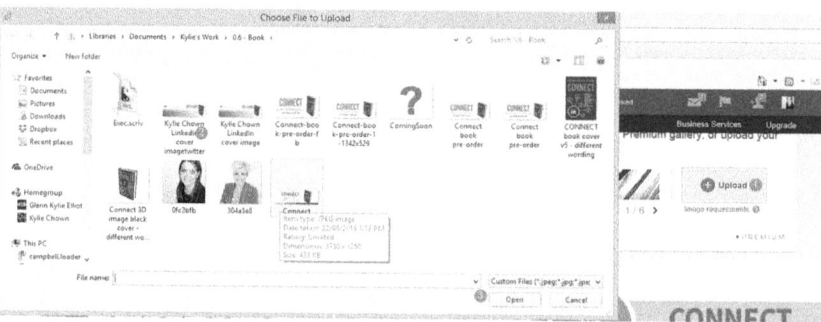

1. Select +upload.
2. Select your image.
3. Select open.

How Do I Use a Hashtag?

A hashtag enables you to search for information about a specific topic. It looks like this: #.

If I wanted to hashtag the word LinkedIn, it would look like this: #LinkedIn. If something has a hashtag, it is essentially searchable as a topic. Some guidelines for hashtags include:

- Don't include spaces.
- You can include numbers, but not punctuation.
- Use relevant hashtags.

Is There Anything I Shouldn't Do on LinkedIn?

The main thing to remember is that LinkedIn is a public domain with the potential to be seen by anyone. As with all social media, only post content you would be happy for anyone to see.

How Do I Spot a Fake Account?

The signs of fake profiles are varied, but with a little work, you too can become an expert at spotting them. Some of the main points to look for include:

1. They may have a cartoon or a movie character name.
2. The information or profile is written in lower-case letters
3. They often have a career history that doesn't make much sense.
4. Often, the information on their profile is sparse and they seldom have any recommendations or LinkedIn applications. There is usually a lack of education or employment history.
5. Photos can look suspect or may be stock images.

Why Do People Set Up Fake LinkedIn Profiles?

The main culprits of fake profiles are spammers. Their intention is to get hold of your email address and the email addresses of everyone you are connected to. When this is achieved, your inbox will be inundated with annoying spam.

In addition to spammers, there are groups that simply want to capture your name for list building. This means your email address will be misused in different ways, from event promotions to porn sites.

Finally, there are also people who just want to find out more about you. Not because they like the look of your profile picture, but because they are interested in your personal content – all of it. Especially the stuff that is only visible to the people you are connected to.

How Do I Protect My LinkedIn Profile?

Always review your connection requests before accepting and take a few minutes to check their profile details.

If something doesn't feel right, don't accept the request. Look for all the red flags highlighted above. Another option is to reply to them using the LinkedIn user agreement and state: "I generally only connect with people I know. Can you tell me why you want to connect and what you hope to achieve?" If you don't get a response, ignore them.

LinkedIn does provide a remedy for spammers in the form of a flag button that will report a profile as spam. If enough people flag a profile, the site administrators will review it and if they determine it is spam, the user's account will be suspended.

How Do I Control the Settings?

There are a number of ways you can protect your information. Once you are logged into your account, click Privacy and Settings.

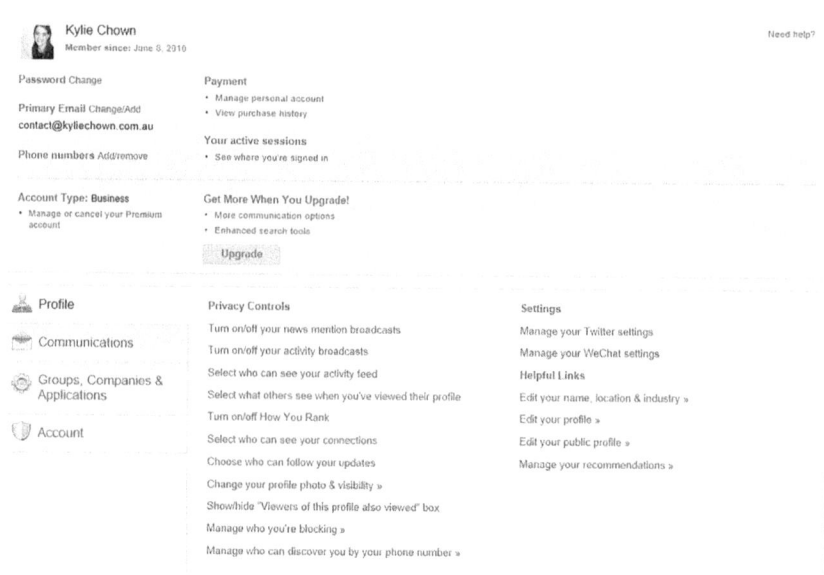

There are a number of primary options here. These include: select who can see your activity feed; see what others see when you have viewed their profile; and manage who you're blocking.

I Am a Consultant/Expert. How Can LinkedIn Help Me?

Forbes recently reported: "By 2020, freelancers will make up 50% of the USA labour force."

We are working with an increasing number of start-up solopreneurs and consultants who are setting up a LinkedIn profile as their number-one step to setting up their business – even before creating a website. LinkedIn is like a whole marketing machine in one place, and you have your blog and database at your fingertips. Setting up a LinkedIn profile is cheap and fast. Consultants can hit the ground running and access their ideal buyers in corporate markets more easily.

I Am a Teacher. How Can LinkedIn Help Me?

Why should teachers be on LinkedIn? In essence, they are brand ambassadors for their school. Kylie recently worked with a school principal who was hesitant to get on LinkedIn, but once Kylie explained that the client's profile was about her school, not her, the client was much more open to engaging on LinkedIn. Ways LinkedIn can help teachers include:

- For school leaders, having their school values in their profile means that prospective students' families that align with these values will be drawn to the school.
- Supports networking and professional development opportunities and allows teachers to develop a collaborative network.
- Validates Google search results and positions teachers as experts in their field.
- Allows the school to celebrate and communicate achievements in a professional manner. We know that LinkedIn is a tool for journalists, so by sharing information on LinkedIn, schools can potentially experience positive media coverage.

Useful Websites

For Finding Keywords: Google Keyword Planner

https://adwords.google.com/KeywordPlanner

Keyword Planner is like a workshop for building new search network campaigns or expanding existing ones. You can search for keyword and ad group ideas, get historical statistics, see how a list of keywords might perform and even create a new keyword list by multiplying several lists of keywords together. A free AdWords tool, Keyword Planner can also help you choose competitive bids and budgets to use with your campaigns.

Top Tip: Even though this is developed for Google AdWords, it is a great research tool for LinkedIn.

For LinkedIn Help: LinkedIn Help Center

https://help.linkedin.com/

Need help using LinkedIn? The LinkedIn Help Center helps you find answers to your questions.

LinkedIn Premium

premium.linkedin.com

For Information on LinkedIn Groups: LinkedIn Group Directory

http://www.linkedin.com/directory/groups

For Different Bullets: Miscellaneous Symbols

http://en.wikipedia.org/wiki/Miscellaneous_Symbols

This is a Unicode block (U+2600–U+26FF) containing glyphs representing concepts from a variety of categories, including astrological, astronomical, chess, dice, musical notation, political symbols, recycling, religious symbols, trigrams, warning signs and weather, among others.

For the CONNECT LinkedIn Group

https://www.linkedin.com/grp/home?gid=7015440

For More Information on Jane Anderson

www.jane-anderson.com

For More Information on Kylie Chown

www.kyliechown.com

Want More Help?

Jane Anderson

Jane is a speaker, author and mentor who works with thought leaders and organisations to help them grow by leveraging their talent and having more impact in their communications. She is a sought-after keynote speaker and contributes regularly to a variety of media publications. Jane holds a Bachelor of Business in Marketing and believes that people buy from people. She has worked as a business consultant and in senior management roles in sales and learning and development.

Some of the areas she can assist your business with include:

- Speaking at conferences and events
- LinkedIn sales strategy for organisations
- Personal branding mentoring
- High-impact presentations

Jane's other publications include:

- **IMPACT:** How to Build Your Personal Brand for the Connection Economy, available on Amazon.com.
- **Understanding Y:** co-authored with Charlie Caruso, published by Wiley. Available on Amazon.com and all other online retail book stores.

She can be found at www.jane-anderson.com

"Jane Anderson is the go-to expert for building your personal brand and with CONNECT, she helps leaders and business owners transform their relationship with LinkedIn from one of awkward and confusing social platform into that of powerful business-building ally."
– Dan Gregory, CEO The Impossible Institute

Kylie Chown

Kylie Chown has been writing LinkedIn profiles and other personally branded communications for consultants, thought leaders and executives for more than 10 years. She works with people so that they have more choice in their businesses and careers. Kylie works with individuals, consultants and business and can assist you with:

- LinkedIn profile development
- LinkedIn coaching
- Resume writing for executives
- Job search strategy and coaching

Kylie has been featured in Australian Institute of Management (AIM), Franchise Business, HRM America and Leaders in Heels.

She is currently one of eight Certified Master Writers in Australia and one of three Reach Certified Branding Analysts.

She can be found at www.kyliechown.com

"Kylie helped me to understand the complexity of LinkedIn profile development, from developing a SEO strategy to having a profile that positions me and the business in a way that supports our future goals. This combined with the coaching means that I can now leverage LinkedIn to represent and support the business in a proactive manner."
– David McDonald, Chief Executive Officer

www.ingramcontent.com/pod-product-compliance
Ingram Content Group UK Ltd.
Pitfield, Milton Keynes, MK11 3LW, UK
UKHW051652180426
11947UKWH00021B/1923